Evolutionary Economics and Social Complexity Science

Volume 21

The Japanese Association for Evolutionary Economics (JAFEE) always has adhered to its original aim of taking an explicit "integrated" approach. This path has been followed steadfastly since the Association's establishment in 1997 and, as well, since the inauguration of our international journal in 2004. We have deployed an agenda encompassing a contemporary array of subjects including but not limited to: foundations of institutional and evolutionary economics, criticism of mainstream views in the social sciences, knowledge and learning in socio-economic life, development and innovation of technologies, transformation of industrial organizations and economic systems, experimental studies in economics, agent-based modeling of socio-economic systems, evolution of the governance structure of firms and other organizations, comparison of dynamically changing institutions of the world, and policy proposals in the transformational process of economic life. In short, our starting point is an "integrative science" of evolutionary and institutional views. Furthermore, we always endeavor to stay abreast of newly established methods such as agent-based modeling, socio/econo-physics, and network analysis as part of our integrative links.

More fundamentally, "evolution" in social science is interpreted as an essential key word, i.e., an integrative and /or communicative link to understand and re-domain various preceding dichotomies in the sciences: ontological or epistemological, subjective or objective, homogeneous or heterogeneous, natural or artificial, selfish or altruistic, individualistic or collective, rational or irrational, axiomatic or psychological-based, causal nexus or cyclic networked, optimal or adaptive, micro- or macroscopic, deterministic or stochastic, historical or theoretical, mathematical or computational, experimental or empirical, agent-based or socio/econo-physical, institutional or evolutionary, regional or global, and so on. The conventional meanings adhering to various traditional dichotomies may be more or less obsolete, to be replaced with more current ones vis-á-vis contemporary academic trends. Thus we are strongly encouraged to integrate some of the conventional dichotomies.

These attempts are not limited to the field of economic sciences, including management sciences, but also include social science in general. In that way, understanding the social profiles of complex science may then be within our reach. In the meantime, contemporary society appears to be evolving into a newly emerging phase, chiefly characterized by an information and communication technology (ICT) mode of production and a service network system replacing the earlier established factory system with a new one that is suited to actual observations. In the face of these changes we are urgently compelled to explore a set of new properties for a new socio/economic system by implementing new ideas. We thus are keen to look for "integrated principles" common to the above-mentioned dichotomies throughout our serial compilation of publications. We are also encouraged to create a new, broader spectrum for establishing a specific method positively integrated in our own original way.

More information about this series at http://www.springer.com/series/11930

Hiroyasu Inoue

Co-patenting: An Analytic Tool for Cooperative Research and Development

Springer

Hiroyasu Inoue
Graduate School of Simulation Studies
University of Hyogo
Kobe, Japan

ISSN 2198-4204 ISSN 2198-4212 (electronic)
Evolutionary Economics and Social Complexity Science
ISBN 978-4-431-54806-5 ISBN 978-4-431-54807-2 (eBook)
https://doi.org/10.1007/978-4-431-54807-2

This Springer imprint is published by the registered company Springer Japan KK, part of Springer Nature.
The registered company address is: Shiroyama Trust Tower, 4-3-1 Toranomon, Minato-ku, Tokyo 105-6005, Japan

Preface

Technological development, or innovation (defined narrowly), is important for sustainable economic growth, and this has been the case throughout human history. In addition, the pace of technological development has grown continuously over time. Therefore, actors such as individuals or organizations must steadily find a better way to create innovation on a constant basis.

Modern society has developed infrastructure, such as transportation systems, the Internet, and novel communication devices. Our society has also adapted to exploiting infrastructure development for innovation. Therefore, where innovations are located and how this has changed over time are important aspects of innovative activities. In addition, the way in which innovations are created has changed to involve multiple actors because combinations of specialties and ideas can create higher-quality innovations more rapidly than can individual actors. Observing and understanding such collaborations can help us to understand the economy and craft policies to encourage innovation.

We need microdata to observe the locations of and collaborations in innovation processes. Although surveys that include a limited number of observations may provide some findings, cost constraints mean that surveys are normally limited to hundreds or thousands of respondents, which are not enough to obtain a macro perspective. Considering that modern society is characterized by broad and ubiquitous relationships and the complex behaviour they generate, such approaches using limited data can only reveal case studies or anecdotes. On the other hand, patent data include massive amounts of information on invention activity, including information on actors' locations and collaborations. In addition, the data are longitudinal, which means that it is possible to study the dynamics of such activity over time.

However, note that there are limitations to using patent data to study the locations and collaborations involved in innovation. First, the data reflect only some innovative activities. Specifically, actors make a strategic decision to patent inventions or to keep them secret. Additionally, if an invention is incomplete, no patent is filed. Moreover, while co-patenting is an indicator of collaborations, not all collaborative research and development efforts ultimately yield co-patenting because a patent may be published by a solo inventor or applicant if the members of the collaborative effort have previously agreed on this approach.

This book compiles a series of my studies on the geographical location and co-patenting using patent data, which were published in eight academic journal articles. Through this book, my hope is that the reader will develop ideas of how we can utilize patent data to understand the geographical embeddedness of innovative actors and how they collaborate as a social behaviour.

Kobe, Japan
September 2019

Hiroyasu Inoue

Acknowledgments

Although writing this book was more difficult than I had expected, it has also been an excellent opportunity to look back on what I have done. I would like to thank Professor Yuji Aruka and Professor Hideaki Aoyama for giving me this precious opportunity.

I have had wonderful collaborators on the works contained in this book, and without them, the book never could have been completed. Professor Kentaro Nakajima gave me considerable advice, despite that he is much younger than me. His broad interest and techniques in economics represent the core of this book. I would like to thank Professor Yukiko Saito for her abundant energy. She has always had paid attention to quality and seen the potential in my work. Professor Yang-Yu Liu gave me a precious opportunity for collaboration when I was at Northeastern University. Professor Wataru Souma kindly taught me the basics of network science. Without his support, I could not have completed the series of works included in this book. Professor Schumpeter Tamada kindly gave me advice on using the patent data.

Beyond the direct collaborators on the works in this book, other important people have been crucial to this work. I thank Professor Hiroshi Iyetomi, Professor Thomas Lux, Professor Yoshi Fujiwara, and Professor Yasuyuki Todo for their kind support. Additionally, I had excellent discussions with people at the Research Institute of Economy, Trade, and Industry, University of Kiel, and University of Hyogo. I truly appreciate their assistance.

I have postponed the deadline of this book so many times. Even so, Mr. Yutaka Hirachi kindly had the patience to wait for my slow writing. I would like to thank him very much.

Contents

Chapter 1
Introduction

Our societies have shifted from labor-intensive to knowledge-intensive economies, and thus, firms consider knowledge to be the essence of competitiveness [26, 31, 44] and must strive to determine how they can create knowledge [14, 24, 55]. Although knowledge is ultimately created by individuals [16], we can consider different levels of actors, not only individuals but also organizations or groups of them [55]. Since actors are influenced by outside factors, studying what elements affect actors and how is an important issue.

One such element is the geographical location of actors. Since geographical distance can be an obstacle to communication, it is natural to assess whether knowledge creation exhibits geographical concentration. The agglomeration of information technology firms in Silicon Valley is a well-known example of such concentration. As other examples, most manufacturing firms in the United Kingdom and Japan tend to be localized [17, 47]. Although such agglomerations are outcomes of many economic factors, the agglomeration of high-performing firms in Silicon Valley implies that one of the most plausible drivers of agglomeration is communication [18, 43, 59]. On the other hand, as information technology advances, it becomes easier for individuals to communicate with one another over long distances. This means that the distance frictions noted above may disappear [10]. In addition, empirical results indicate that the barriers imposed by international borders, which represent a typical geographical friction, have recently declined [27]. Therefore, the issue of distance requires careful investigation.

A localization per se does not indicate which actors communicate with one another. On the other hand, if we observe concrete relationships, i.e. collaborations between actors, we can directly investigate the geographical friction involved in communication, and more important, we can consider indirect relationships among actors. Since collaboration increases the likelihood of innovation [62], enables firms to utilize external knowledge [12, 40], and accelerates innovations [26, 67], greater attention has recently been paid to studying collaboration [55], and firms take collaborations seriously [30]. Although a genius could develop great innovations [9],

H. Inoue, *Co-patenting: An Analytic Tool for Cooperative Research and Development*, Evolutionary Economics and Social Complexity Science 21,
https://doi.org/10.1007/978-4-431-54807-2_1

recent studies show that teams can generate better outcomes than individuals, on average [68], and have also revealed an increasing propensity for team rather than individual-based innovation [36, 45, 68].

We can analyse the localizations of collaborations by using data with regional aggregation [34, 53]. However, since some studies contend that knowledge spillovers occur over short distances [4, 37, 60], we expect collaborations to occur within areas smaller than administrative regions. Therefore, such regionally aggregated data are insufficient to study collaboration geography. We thus need to utilize collaboration data with microgeography and measures capable of handling such data [17, 41, 42].

Another important aspect of collaboration is networks. There is an extensive literature on collaboration networks [56]. However, while these studies tend to use the term "network", most consider only bilateral relationships. A network and its analysis are applicable only where it is necessary to consider indirect connections. This means that we consider more complex network structures rather than bilateral relationships. For example, works that study networks properly discuss how knowledge is propagated to indirectly connected firms through directly connected firms [20–23, 25]. Unlike bilateral relationships, networks enable us to examine structural attributes by using network centrality measures. In addition, we can also discuss densely connected components of networks, i.e. communities. These new dimensions allow us to study how complex relationships affect innovations.

We can examine various actors involved in innovation processes. These are individuals (i.e. developers or researchers), groups, business establishments, and firms. These different types of actors can affect one another. For example, individuals in different firms appear to collaborate because of past collaborations between firms even if those previous collaborative efforts involved different individuals. Therefore, we can even consider the interdependency of multilayered collaborations. In addition, if collaborating individuals belong to different firms, we expect greater frictions or difficulty in their efforts to collaborate [32, 52] because there may be conflicts of interest and the risk of leaking confidential information. However, such frictions may be mitigated if collaborations occur over a short geographic distance.

Firms collaborate because they expect to obtain external knowledge. This is simply because different firms tend to have different impactful knowledge. However, even if collaborations are successful a given moment, outcomes can change over time if collaborations are long-lasting. Although actors can cultivate mutual relationships and improve performance through collaboration [38, 61], how they should deepen their relationships can be an issue. As the length of a collaboration increases, it becomes more likely that the knowledge of the actors involved becomes similar and less new knowledge can be exchanged. Therefore, collaborations can degenerate or decline in quality. In other words, repeat collaborations perform worse than initial collaborations. The literature from many fields finds that collaborations impair creativity, such as scientific research [29, 54], consulting practice [58], and entertainment performances [15, 29, 51, 66]. This phenomenon has been termed "creative abrasion" [63]. However, how collaboration on innovation changes over time has received limited attention.

This book employs several decades of US and Japanese patent records [1, 2, 39, 64] to study the issues raised above. Patent records enable us to study long-term and large-scale data. Since a patent application must meet certain criteria such as novelty and non-obviousness and facilitates and encourages the disclosure of innovations in the public domain, patent records can be considered direct evidence of innovations over time [19, 21, 28]. Importantly, the data contain over one million records and hundreds of thousands of actors. Collecting the same amount of information via a survey would be prohibitively expensive and would be lacking in the temporal dimension. Another considerable advantage of using patent records is that we can extract information on different levels of actors. A patent application can be filed by multiple inventors and/or multiple firms.

Moreover, we can extract establishment information from Japanese patent data. Such information is particularly helpful in identifying the exact place where the R&D activity actually occurred. In the literature on knowledge spillovers, patent data have been investigated at the inventor level [35, 37, 46, 65]. However, inventors' addresses are normally their residential addresses rather than the addresses of their workplaces. Therefore, the address does not represent the place where the invention and interaction actually occurred. One could conduct firm-level analysis using the address of a firm's headquarters, but these addresses are unsuitable for studying the locations of inventions. Because firms can have multiple establishments, headquarters addresses do not necessarily represent the actual locations of inventions. On the other hand, since Japanese patent data on the addresses registered by inventors include the addresses of establishments instead of the addresses of their residences, we can construct establishment-level data on Japanese patent records.

Despite the difficulties in overcoming gaps related to firm climates and the intangibility of knowledge [50], firms have increasingly pursued collaborations [12, 26, 40] to utilize other firms' knowledge. Commensurate with this, co-patenting by multiple actors has increased [33]. Since co-patenting strongly indicates collaborations between actors and the patent records have long-term coverage and large samples, co-patenting is a very powerful tool to study collaborative activities in innovation. Moreover, the patent records and the co-authorship enable us to analyse networks that indicate how actors indirectly affect one another.

Although we investigate co-patenting to identify collaborations between actors, patent citations are often used in the literature on knowledge spillovers [27, 35, 37, 46, 65]. Citations obviously indicate codified knowledge transfers but do not necessarily mean collaborations between actors. This is because if a patent is published, any inventor can cite it in his or her subsequent patent. In contrast to citations, co-patenting directly indicates collaborations. Even tacit knowledge can be transferred if inventors collaborate.

Using patent records also enables us to analyse repeat collaborations. Since patent records have rich data on repeat collaborations, we can discuss this issue in greater detail than has previously been possible.

Although co-patenting is evidence of collaborations between actors, the opposite is not true. Namely, when actors collaborate, they do not in most cases publish patents. This is a limitation of our approach. However, it does, as noted above, have the clear advantage that we can use many observations over time with many actors. Additionally, patent records represent the strongest available approach to study the issues discussed in this chapter.

An actor's location is an important concern throughout this book. The geocoding service provided by the Center for Spatial Information Science of the University of Tokyo is used herein to convert addresses in Japanese patent data to longitudes and latitudes. Since this identification is highly precise, we can even identify whether establishments are located in the same or a neighbouring building. As noted above, data at a regional aggregation are insufficient to study the distances between actors. Therefore, accurate locations of actors are necessary to obtain the distances between them, which then enables us to discuss geographic proximity, an important topic of this book.

Although we can obtain the distribution of the distances between actors in general, note that there is also geographic proximity between overall locations. This is because cities have large populations and actors are also localized [3, 11]. Therefore, we need to control for overall proximity. To do so, we employ the K-density approach developed by Duranton and Overman [17] to avoid bias derived from overall aggregation, although another method has also been advocated [41, 42]. This approach can create a confidence band through bootstrapping. By applying this approach to data from different periods, we can also discuss whether information technology eliminates distance as a barrier to research activities. In addition, by separating the data into inter-firm collaborations and intra-firm collaborations, we can address the firm-border effect. Moreover, by separating the data by firm size, we can examine how the size of firms affects the distance involved in collaborations. Finally, we apply our approach to different technological categories to identify how aggregations occur over short distances in the high-tech sector, for example.

Knowledge can be indirectly propagated through firms via collaborations [20–23, 25]. As noted above, we can create networks through co-patenting. Unlike bilateral relationships, networks are abstracts of complex systems and reflect complex behaviour. Since networks are observed in many different areas, from protein interaction to human society, there is a literature on this topic, which is named network science [5]. Network science consists of theory based on physics and numerous empirical findings. It reports common features of networks in different fields and models to replicate these features.

By accounting for networks, we can obtain a higher concept of systems. Some components of networks are densely connected, while other components are not. We expect that more knowledge circulates in highly connected components (communities) than in other components. Furthermore, additional research questions on communities can be addressed. One such question is what nodes constitute communities. Geographic circumstances may affect the growth of communities, in line with the discussion in this chapter. In addition, knowledge differences between nodes may also affect community growth. Actors collaborate to share their unique knowledge, but if their knowledge is completely different, they cannot collaborate, and if most of the knowledge held by actors is the same, they will be less likely to create new ideas [8].

Since collaborations grant actors access to outside knowledge, it is beneficial to know when actors collaborate with others. Regression models, which despite being commonly used, have weaknesses regarding endogeneity and are thus are not suitable for modelling such behaviour. For example, an actor with excellent innovation ability attracts more co-patenting. Moreover, an actor engaged in more co-patenting acquires more innovation. This mutual causality clearly demonstrates the endogeneity issue. Most likely, both effects exist, and regression models cannot address this issue. Instead, network science has proposed many generative models to replicate networks. For example, it is well known that the likelihood of a node acquiring a new link is proportional to the links the node has acquired in the past [7]. If a model can replicate networks well by adjusting its parameters, the model can be used to understand the replication mechanism. As we need substantial empirical network data to verify a model, we have a large dataset, and this approach is thus applicable.

We can create a generative model that only incorporates nodes and links, which means that which nodes are connected is determined solely by the links they have. However, since the focus in this book is a detailed consideration of the geographic aspects of collaborations, we create a model with both features, i.e. the number of links and the distance between nodes.

Although many generative models have been proposed [6, 48, 49, 57], previous studies focus on one-layer networks. In this book, actors can be inventors, business establishments, or firms. These actors are network nodes, and the links are collaborations between them. Normally, we only consider one type of actor as a network node, such as in inventor networks. However, a considerable advantage of the patent data is that the actors have nested relationships. Namely, inventors belong to business establishments, and business establishments belong to firms. Therefore, we can discuss how such hierarchical relationships are observed in networks and how such relationships affect the growth of the networks. Although some prior studies have investigated two-layered networks and proposed a model [13], it uses overall information, which is unrealistic in complex networks.

Although we do not use regression models to replicate collaboration networks, regression models remain useful to develop a general understanding of what actor attributes affect actors' interactions. Therefore, we employ regression models in this book where helpful.

This book proceeds as follows. Chapter 2 describes the characteristics of co-patenting networks, and Chap. 3 discusses how long inventors should maintain a collaboration and when they should leave it. Chapters 4 and 5 examine the distance between establishments and their collaborations, respectively. Chapter 6 discusses communities of establishments. Finally, Chaps. 7 and 8 address generative models.

References

1. http://www.japio.or.jp/english/
2. http://www.nber.org/
3. Arbia G, Espa G, Quah D. A class of spatial econometric methods in the empirical analysis of clusters of firms in the space. Empir Econ. 2008;34(1):81–103.
4. Arzaghi M, Henderson JV. Networking off Madison avenue. Rev Econ Stud. 2008;75(4):1011–38.
5. Barabási A-L. Network science. New York: Cambridge University Press; 2016.
6. Barabási AL, Albert R. Statistical mechanics of complex networks. Rev Mod Phys. 2002;74:47–97.
7. Barabási AL, Oltvai ZN. Network biology: understanding the cell's functional organization. Nat Rev Genet. 2004;5:101–13.
8. Berliant M, Fujita M. Knowledge creation as a square dance on the Hilbert cube. Int Econ Rev. 2008;49(4):1251–95.
9. Bowler PJ, Morus IR. Making modern science: a historical survey. Chicago: University of Chicago Press; 2005.
10. Cairncross F. The death of distance: how the communications revolution is changing our lives. Boston: Harvard Business School Press; 2001. ISBN: 9781578514380.
11. Carlino GA, et al. The agglomeration of R&D labs. Working Paper Series 12–22. Federal Reserve Bank of Philadelphia; 2012.
12. Chesbrough HW. Open innovation. Boston: Harvard Business School; 2003.
13. Chessa A, et al. Is Europe evolving toward an integrated research area? Science. 2013;339(6120):650–1.
14. Czarnitzki D. An empirical test of the asymmetric models on innovative activity: who invests more into R&D, the incumbent or the challenger? J Econ Behav Organ. 2004;54(2):153–73.
15. Delmestri G, Montanari F, Usai A. Reputation and strength of ties in predicting commercial success and artistic merit of independents in the italian feature film industry*. J Manage Stud. 2005;42(5):975–1002.
16. Drucker P. The age of discontinuity: guidelines to our changing society. New Brunswick: Transaction Publishers; 1992.
17. Duranton G, Overman HG. Testing for localization using micro-geographic data. Rev Econ Stud. 2005;72(4):1077–106.
18. Ellison G, Glaeser EL, Kerr WR. What causes industry agglomeration? Am Econ Rev. 2010;105:889–927.
19. Fleming L, Sorenson O. Technology as a complex adaptive system: evidence from patent data. Res Policy. 2001;30:1019–39.
20. Fleming L, King III C, Juda AI. Small worlds and regional innovation. Org Sci. 2007;18(6):938–54.
21. Fleming L, Mingo S, Chen D. Collaborative brokerage, generative creativity, and creative success. Adm Sci Q. 2007;52(3):443–75.
22. Forti E, Franzoni C, Sobrero M. Bridges or isolates? Investigating the social networks of academic inventors. Res Policy 2013;42(8):1378–88.
23. Gautam A. Collaboration networks, structural holes, and innovation: a longitudinal study. Adm Sci Q. 2000;45(3):425–55.
24. Geroski P, Machin S, Reenen JV. The profitability of innovating firms. RAND J Econ. 1993;24(2):198–211.
25. Gonzalez-Brambila CN, Veloso FM, Krackhardt D. The impact of network embeddedness on research output. Res Policy. 2013;42(9):1555–67.
26. Grant RM. Toward a knowledge-based theory of the firm. Strateg Manag J. 1996;17:109–22.
27. Griffith R, Lee S, Van Reenen J. Is distance dying at last? Falling home bias in fixed-effects models of patent citations. Quant Econ. 2011;2(2):211–49.

28. Griliches Z. R&D and productivity-the economic evidence. Chicago: The University of Chicago Press; 1998.
29. Guimera R, et al. Team assembly mechanisms determine collaboration network structure and team performance. Science. 2005;308(5722):697–702.
30. Hagedoorn J, Kranenburg HV, Osborn RN. Joint patenting amongst companies – exploring the effects of interfirm R&D partnering and experience. Manag Decis Econ. 2003;24:71–84.
31. Hall BH, Jaffe AB, Trajtenberg M. The NBER patent citations data file: lessons, insights and methodological tools. National Bureau of Economic Research Working Paper 8498. 2001.
32. Hausler J, Hohn H-W, Lutz S, et al. Contingencies of innovative networks: a case study of successful interfirm R&D collaboration. Res Policy. 1994;23(1):47–66.
33. Hicks D, et al. Research excellence and patented innovation. Sci Public Policy. 2000;27(5):310–20.
34. Hoekman J, Frenken K, Van Oort F. The geography of collaborative knowledge production in Europe. Ann Reg Sci. 2009;43(3):721–38.
35. Jaffe AB, Trajtenberg M, Henderson R. Geographic localization of knowledge spillovers as evidenced by patent citations. Q J Econ. 1993;108(3):577–98.
36. Jones BF. The burden of knowledge and the 'Death of the renaissance man': is innovation getting harder? NBER Working Paper Series. 2005.
37. Kerr WR, Kominers SD. Agglomerative forces and cluster shapes. Rev Econ Stat. 2015;97(4):877–99.
38. Kozlowski SWJ, Bell BS. Work groups and teams in organizations. In: Borman WC, Ilgen DR, Klimoski RJ, editors. Handbook of psychology. New York: Wiley; 2003, vol. 12, p. 333–75.
39. Lai R, D'Amour A, Yu A, Sun Y, Fleming L. Disambiguation and Co-authorship Networks of the U.S. Patent Inventor Database (1975–2010); 2011.
40. Laursen K, Salter A. Open for innovation: the role of openness in explaining innovation performance among U.K. manufacturing firms. Strateg Manag J. 2006;27(2):131–50.
41. Marcon E, Puech F. Evaluating the geographic concentration of industries using distance-based methods. J Econ Geogr. 2003;3(4):409–28.
42. Marcon E, Puech F. Measures of the geographic concentration of industries: improving distance-based methods. J Econ Geogr. 2010;10(5):745–62.
43. Marshall A. Principles of economics. London: Macmillan; 1920.
44. McEvily SK, Chakravarthy B. The persistence of knowledge-based advantage: an empirical test for product performance and technological knowledge. Strateg Manag J. 2002;23(4):285–305.
45. Merton RK. The sociology of science: theoretical and empirical investigations. Chicago: University of Chicago Press; 1979.
46. Murata Y, et al. Localized knowledge spillovers and patent citations: a distance-based approach. Rev Econ Stat. 2014;96(5):967–85.
47. Nakajima K, Saito YU, Uesugi I. Localization of interfirm transaction relationships and industry agglomeration. RIETI Discussion Paper Series, 12-E-23. 2012.
48. Newman MEJ. The structure of scientific collaboration networks. Proc Nat Acad Sci USA. 2001;98:404–9.
49. Newman MEJ. Coauthorship networks and patterns of scientific collaboration. Proc Nat Acad Sci USA. 2004;101:5200–5.
50. Nonaka I, Lewin AY. A dynamic theory of organizational knowledge creation. Org Sci. 1994;5(1):14–37.
51. Perretti F, Negro G. Mixing genres and matching people: a study in innovation and team composition in Hollywood. J Organ Behav. 2007;586:563–86.
52. Pittaway L, et al. Networking and innovation: a systematic review of the evidence. Int J Manag Rev. 2004;5(3–4):137–68.
53. Ponds R, Van Oort F, Frenken K. The geographical and institutional proximity of research collaboration. Pap Reg Sci. 2007;86(3):423–43.
54. Porac JF, et al. Human capital heterogeneity, collaborative relationships, and publication patterns in a multidisciplinary scientific alliance: a comparative case study of two scientific

teams. Res Policy. 2004;33(4):661–78. ISSN: 0048-7333. https://doi.org/10.1016/j.respol.2004.01.007.
55. Porter ME. On competition. Boston: Harvard Business School Press; 1998.
56. Powell WW, Grodal S. The Oxford handbook of innovation, Chap. 3. Oxford: Oxford University Press; 2006. p. 56–85.
57. Ramasco J, Dorogovtsev S, Pastor-Satorras R. Self-organization of collaboration networks. Phys Rev E. 2004;70(30):1–10.
58. Reagans R, Zuckerman E, McEvily B. How to make the team: social networks vs. demography as criteria for designing effective teams. Adm Sci Q. 2004;49(1):101–33.
59. Rosenthal SS, Strange WC. The determinants of agglomeration. J Urban Econ. 2001;50(2):191–229.
60. Rosenthal SS, Strange WC. Geography, industrial organization, and agglomeration. Rev Econ Stat. 2003;85(2):377–93.
61. Schwab A, Miner AS. Learning in hybrid-project systems: the effects of project performance on repeated collaboration. Acad Manag J. 2008;51:1117–49.
62. Simonton DK. Scientific genius: a psychology of science. Cambridge: Cambridge University Press; 1988.
63. Skilton PF, Dooley KJ. The effects of repeat collaboration on creative abrasion. Acad Manag Rev. 2010;35(1):118–134. ISSN: 0363-7425. https://doi.org/10.5465/AMR.2010.45577886.
64. Tamada S, Kodama F, Gemba K. A study on science linkage of Japanese patents; an analysis on patents in the field of genetic technology by constructing a citation database. J Sci Policy Res Manag. 2002;17(3/4):222–30.
65. Thompson P, Fox-Kean M. Patent citations and the geography of knowledge spillovers: a reassessment. Am Econ Rev. 2005;95(1):450–60.
66. Uzzi B, Spiro J. Collaboration and creativity: the small world problem. Am J Sociol. 2005;111(2):447–504.
67. Weisberg RW. Creativity: understanding innovation in problem solving, science, invention, and the arts. New York: Wiley; 2006.
68. Wuchty S, Jones BF, Uzzi B. The increasing dominance of teams in production of knowledge. Science. 2007;316(5827):1036–9.

Chapter 2
Collaboration Networks on Inventors and Firms

2.1 Introduction

This chapter discusses collaborations between inventors and firms and their networks for doing so. The findings in this chapter mainly rely on the author's past works [16, 18]. Most texts, figures, and tables are reproduced under the Creative Commons Attribution License or with proper permission from the publisher. The main text is modified to fit the context of this book.

As noted in Chap. 1, how innovations are created is important for economic growth [26]. Collaboration is key for innovation because collaboration increases the likelihood of combinations of ideas that may result in an innovative and valuable product [30]. For example, an inventor might combine his or her half idea with another inventor's half idea to create a whole innovative idea. Moreover, collaboration can accelerate the delivery of innovations [40], which may involve the parallel validation of initial conceptions and the serial implementation of final ideas. Since speed is the last great competitive advantage for innovations, the greater speed gained through collaboration could be a crucial determinant of the success of creative enterprises. While collaboration has been considered a central theme in innovation, how the effect of collaboration on innovation changes over time has not been quantitatively and systematically studied.

Previous studies find that repeat collaborations usually underperform in creative projects, e.g. scientific research [13, 25], consulting practice [29], and entertainment performances [6, 13, 24, 37]. These interesting results are explained by the hindrance imposed by "creative abrasion" (a sequence of processes constituted by idea generation, disclosure/advocacy, and convergence), which is key to creative project performance [32]. Despite these intriguing results on the negative relationship between repeat collaboration and team performance, the effect of repeat collaboration on innovation is not yet fully understood.

H. Inoue, *Co-patenting: An Analytic Tool for Cooperative Research and Development*, Evolutionary Economics and Social Complexity Science 21,
https://doi.org/10.1007/978-4-431-54807-2_2

This analysis considers Japanese and US patent records from several decades [1, 2, 14, 19, 33] to demonstrate the effect of collaboration on innovation. Patent records are valuable for this research. First, the purpose of patents is to facilitate and encourage the disclosure of innovations in the public domain for the common good. A typical patent application must meet the relevant patentability requirements such as novelty and non-obviousness. Hence, patent records are directly related to the occurrence of innovations over time [9, 10, 12]. We can track and analyse innovation activity over long periods of time by mining patent records. In contrast to patent records, team performance in scientific research, consulting practice, and the entertainment industry cannot always be directly related to innovation. For example, scientific findings, especially in fundamental science, do not always lead to more effective products or technologies that are readily available to markets and society. Second, there are two levels of collaboration in patent records. A patent application can be filed by multiple inventors and/or multiple firms. Although different firms can have different corporate climates and unique tacit knowledge [22], firms are increasingly capitalizing on other firms knowledge to accelerate innovation [5, 11, 20]. Commensurate with this trend, the number of joint patents applied for by multiple firms continues to exhibit an increasing trend [15]. Since innovations can be driven by the collaborations of inventors and/or firms, it would be very interesting to study the effect of collaboration on innovation at both the inventor and firm levels.

A collection of collaborations is a collaboration network. If we examine the collective structure, we can derive new findings that cannot be obtained by examining each bilateral collaboration. In this respect, numerous extensive studies in social science have analysed innovation based on networks [27]. However, these studies have focused on small-scale networks and have only examined a thousand firms at most. By contrast, this chapter considers large networks based on patents.

2.2 Collaboration Networks

A patent can be requested by filing an application. Inventors and/or firms can apply for patents. In this work, we analyse Japanese and US patent records (accessible from http://www.iip.or.jp/e/ and http://www.nber.org/, respectively), which cover different years and different numbers of inventors and firms.

We first study the structure of the underlying collaboration networks to assess the similarity and/or difference of two patent records. We then construct a collaboration network of inventors (or firms) by drawing a link between two nodes i and j if they collaborated at least once, i.e. they filed at least one patent application together (see Fig. 2.1), where nodes are inventors (or firms) and links represent the collaborations between inventors (or firms) [8]. The total number of collaborators for node i is called its degree, denoted k_i. The total number of collaborations

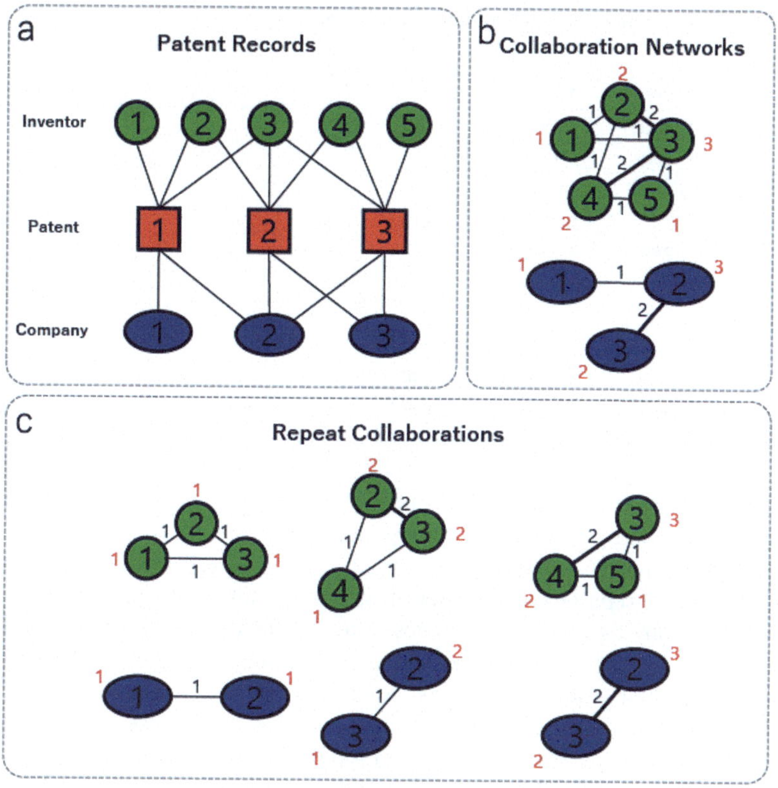

Fig. 2.1 Patent records and the associated collaboration networks. (**a**) Patent records contain collaborations at both the inventor and firm levels. (**b**) By drawing a undirected link between nodes i and j if they filed a patent application at least once, we can construct the collaboration networks of inventors (or firms). The total number of collaborations between nodes i and j over the whole patent record is defined as the weight of the link (i, j) (shown in black). The total number of collaborators for node i over the whole patent record is defined as the weight of the node i (shown in red). (**c**) The inventors (or firms) listed in each patent record form a clique. For each patent, we calculate the repeat collaboration number ($R_{\rm l}$) for its inventors (or firms) by averaging the accumulated number of collaborations among all the inventor (or firm) pairs in the team (shown in black). The productivity of node i in terms of patents is defined as the accumulated number of patents that node i has contributed. We calculate team productivity ($R_{\rm n}$) by averaging the productivity of all the team's nodes (shown in red). (Source: [16])

between nodes i and j is defined as the weight of the link (i, j), denoted $w_{\rm l}(i, j)$. The total number of patents that node i has contributed to is defined as its weight, denoted $w_{\rm n}(i)$.

Table 2.1 shows the basic information on the Japanese and US patent records and the constructed collaboration networks. The collaboration networks at the inventor and firm levels were constructed based on several decades of Japanese and US patent records, with the number of patents denoted by $N_{\rm P}$. For each collaboration network, we report the number of nodes (N), edges (E), mean degree ($\langle k \rangle = 2E/N$), relative

Table 2.1 Patent records and collaboration networks. (Source: [16])

Patent record							
	Duration	N_P					
Japan	1994–2008	1,967,361					
USA	1963–1999	2,923,922					
Inventor network							
	N	E	$\langle k \rangle$	s_{lc}	n_0	C	r
Japan	1,806,259	3,458,690	3.830	0.358	0.135	0.438	0.333
USA	72,840	70,702	1.941	0.364	0.542	0.068	−0.056
Firm network							
	N	E	$\langle k \rangle$	s_{lc}	n_0	C	r
Japan	1,528,610	2,599,540	3.401	0.453	0.232	0.334	0.151
USA	148,220	15,896	0.214	0.049	0.907	0.041	−0.032

size of the largest connected component ($s_{lc} = N_{lc}/N$, where N_{lc} is the number of nodes in the largest connected component), fraction of isolated nodes (n_0), clustering coefficient (C), and degree correlation (r). In graph theory, the connected components of a graph G form the set of the largest subgraphs of G that are each connected (i.e. any two vertices or nodes in a connected component are connected to one another by paths), which can be easily computed using either breadth-first search or depth-first search. The largest connected component (often referred to as the giant component) is the connected component of the largest size (number of nodes). The clustering coefficient C of a graph is a measure of the degree to which the nodes in the graph tend to cluster together (i.e. form triangles) [39]. C can be calculated as (3 $\times$ the number of triangles)/(the number of connected triples). The degree correlation r of a network is given by the Pearson correlation coefficient of degrees between pairs of linked nodes [21].

At the inventor level, both the Japanese and US collaboration networks show very high clustering coefficients C and high assortative degree correlations r. A high C indicates that inventors tend to cluster together, i.e. two collaborators of an inventor also tend to be collaborators of one another. A high r means that hub inventors (with high degree k) tend to collaborate with other hub inventors. At the firm level, however, both the Japanese and US collaboration networks display very low clustering coefficients ($C \approx 0$) and slightly disassortative degree correlations ($r \lessapprox 0$), which are qualitatively different from the findings for the inventor collaboration networks.

Naturally, those networks are time varying because of the addition of new patents. Hence, the aggregate statistics of the networks constructed from the entire patent records might not be good measures of the networks constructed at a particular point in time. To ensure that the collaboration networks have stabilized to some extent, we calculate seven basic graph characteristics (N, E, $\langle k \rangle$, s_{lc}, n_0, C, and r) of the collaboration networks constructed from the first p fraction of the entire patent records under study that are chronologically ordered, with p tuned from 0.1 to 1.0. (See Fig. 2.2.) We then plot those graph characteristics as functions of p. The results indicate that although the networks are growing (the number of nodes N and number of edges E are increasing) and becoming denser (the mean degree $\langle k \rangle = 2E/N$ is increasing), many other graph characteristics, e.g. the fraction of the largest connected component (s_{lc}), the fraction of isolated nodes (n_0), the average clustering coefficient (C), and the degree correlation (r), are actually exhibiting steady values, especially at the firm level.

Figure 2.3 shows the distributions. Despite that the Japanese and US collaboration networks cover different years and different numbers of inventors and firms, their degree distributions $P(k)$, node weight distributions $P(w_{\mathrm{n}})$, link weight distributions $P(w_{\mathrm{l}})$, and component size distributions $P(S)$ display qualitatively similar features. In addition, they are very stable for $p > 0.6$ at both the inventor and firm levels. These findings prompt us to compare the stable graph characteristics of the Japanese and US collaboration networks.

At the firm level, the Japanese and US collaboration networks display some quantitative differences. For example, they have different fractions of isolated nodes, denoted n_0, that never collaborate with others, specifically, $n_0 = 0.542$ for Japan and 0.907 for the United States. The relative sizes of their largest connected components, denoted s_{lc}, are also different: $s_{\mathrm{lc}} = 0.364$ for Japan and 0.049 for the United States. The large value of s_{lc} in the Japanese firm collaboration network indicates that Japanese firms are highly connected through collaboration. In contrast, the US firms are not well connected in innovative teams. This structural difference is also reflected in their mean degrees ($\langle k \rangle = 1.941$ for Japan and 0.214 for the United States). The high value of n_0 and low values of s_{lc} and $\langle k \rangle$ for the US firm collaboration network imply that firm collaborations in innovation are not very popular in the United States. Note that according to both US (35 U.S.C. 262) and Japanese patent law (Article 73), a firm cannot sell or license a jointly applied patent without the consent of the others involved. However, Japanese firms seems to be more open to collaborating on patents than are US firms.

Calculating the degree correlation is a useful measure when discussing network structure [23]. This is represented by the conditional probability $p_c(k'|k)$, namely, the probability that a link belonging to a node with degree k will be connected to a node with degree k'. If this conditional probability is independent of k, the network has a topology without any correlation between the nodes' degrees. That is, $p_c(k'|k) = p_c(k') \propto k' p(k')$. In contrast, explicit dependence on k reveals nontrivial correlations between nodes' degrees and the possible presence of a hierarchical structure in the network. Directly measuring $p_c(k'|k)$ is a rather complex task due to the large number of links. A useful measure is $< k_{nn} >= \sum_{k'} k' p_c(k'|k)$, i.e. the average degree of neighbouring nodes with degree k. Figure 2.4 depicts the average degree of the network of all nodes. The horizontal axis shows the degree k, and the vertical axis shows the degree correlation $< k_{nn} >$. These values are for the Japanese firm network. Figure 2.4 presents a null correlation. Therefore, we cannot detect the presence of a hierarchical structure for the degree in the network.

Figure 2.5 shows the average clustering coefficient for the network of all nodes with degree k. The horizontal axis indicates degree k, and the vertical axis represents

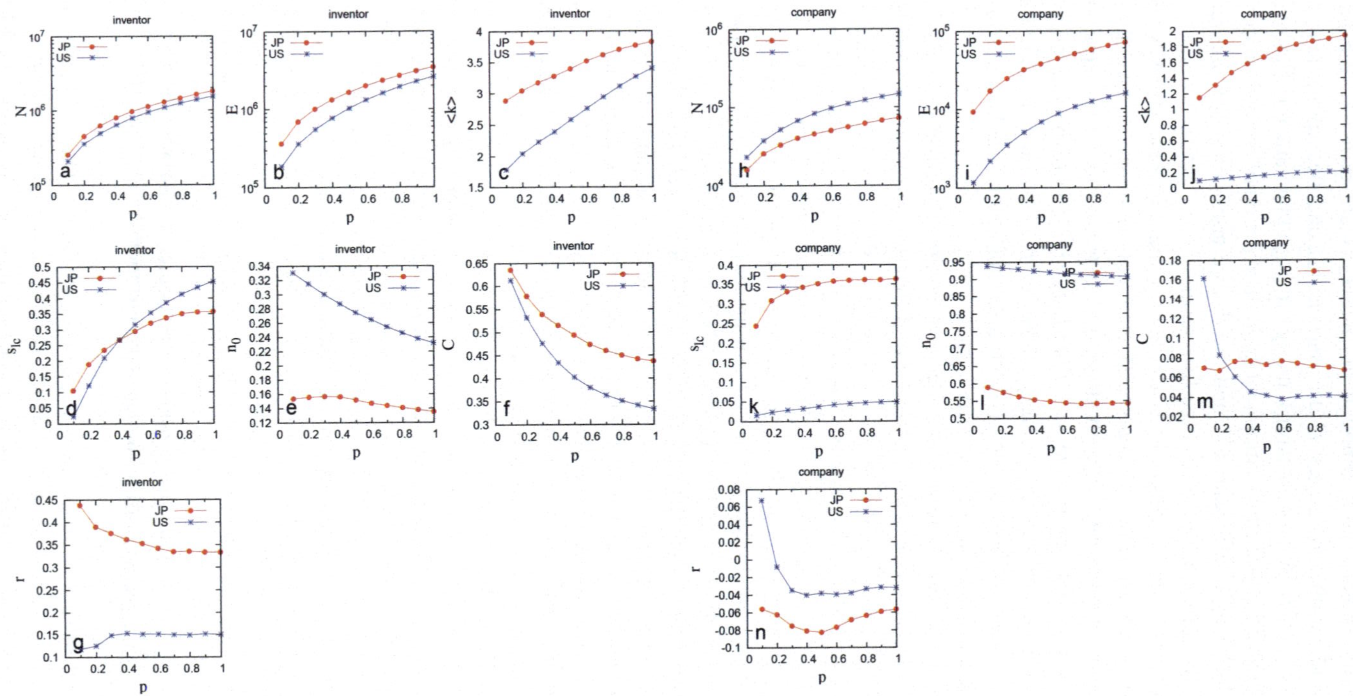

Fig. 2.2 Characteristics of collaboration networks. (**a–g**) Inventors. (**h–n**) firms. The collaboration networks of inventors (or firms) can be constructed from the patent records. (Source: [16])

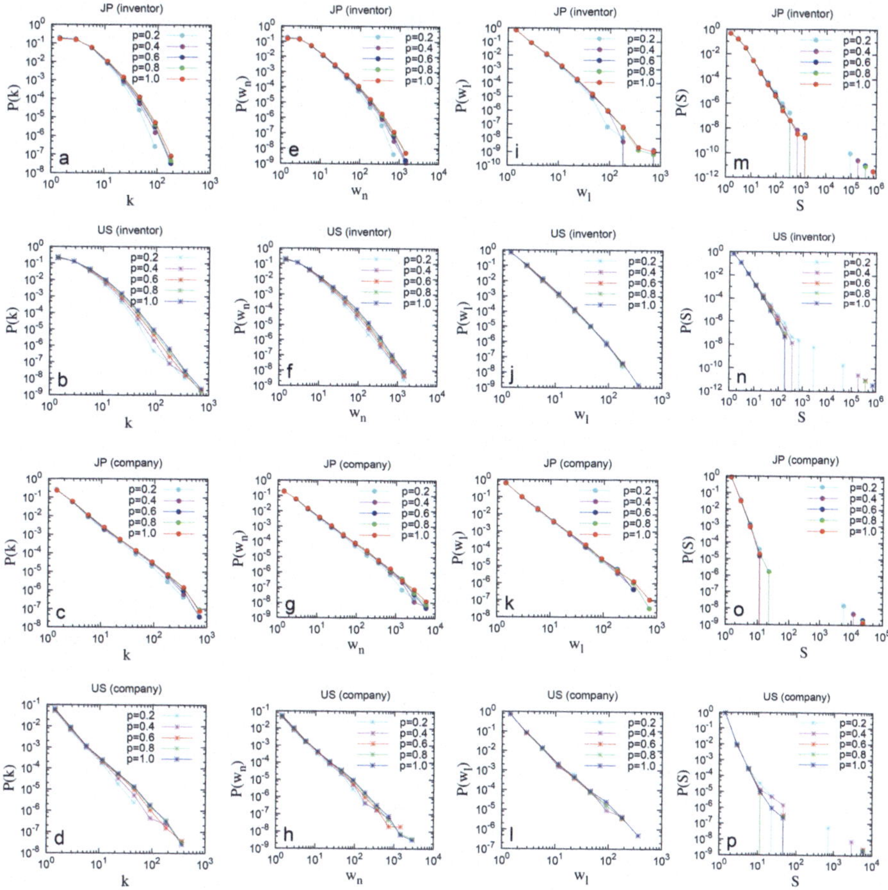

Fig. 2.3 Characteristic distributions of collaboration networks. From left to right: Distributions of node degree (k), node weight (w_n), link weight (w_l), and component size (S). (Source: [16])

the average clustering coefficient, $C(k)$, of all nodes with degree k. There seems to be a negative correlation. If a scale-free network has $C(k) \propto k^{-1}$, the network is hierarchically modular [3]. The hierarchical structure here means that sparsely connected nodes are part of highly clustered areas, with communication between different highly clustered neighbours being maintained by a few hubs. This means that a node may have to traverse redundant hubs to access nodes in other modules.

Figure 2.6 shows the frequency of distance for all links. The horizontal axis represents the geodesic distance, and the vertical axis indicates the frequency. This figure represents the Japanese firm network. The distance of each link is based on the nodes' addresses connected by the link. The addresses are converted into pairs of latitudes and longitudes, and the geodesic distance is calculated from these.

There are several peaks. The largest is at approximately the first 10 km. This peak indicates that the nearer firms are, the more likely they are to have links. However,

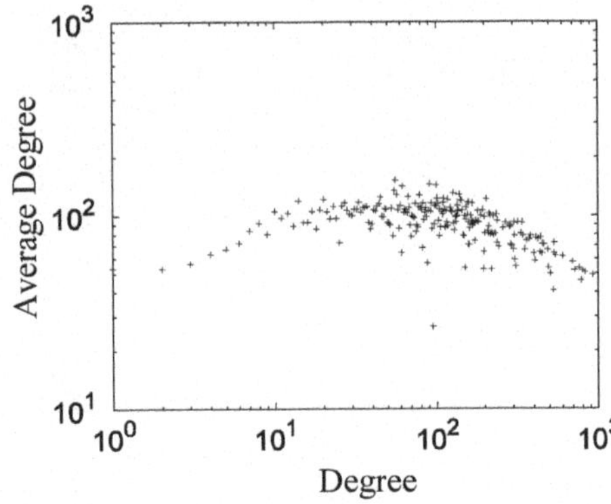

Fig. 2.4 Average degree $< k_{nn} >$. This figure shows nearest neighbours' average degree of nodes with degree k. (Source: [18])

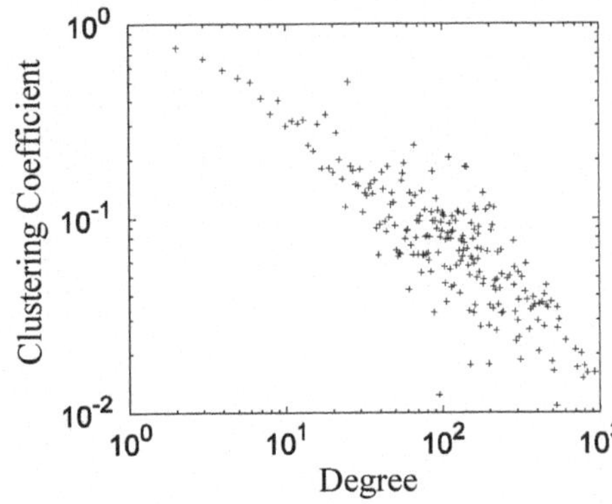

Fig. 2.5 Clustering coefficient $C(k)$. This figure shows the average clustering coefficient of all nodes with degree k. (Source: [18])

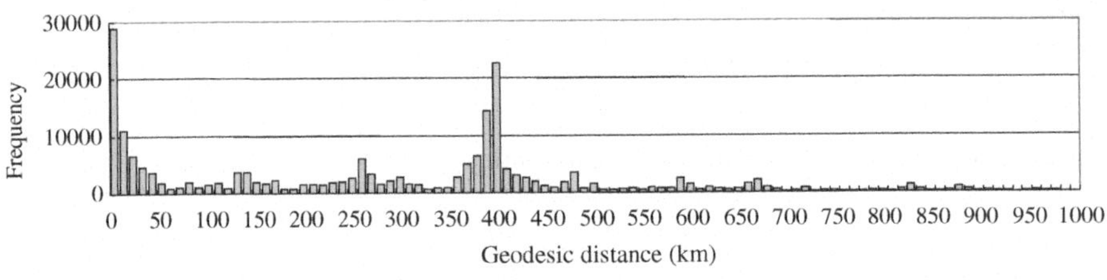

Fig. 2.6 Frequency of distance. Distance of each link is calculated by the addresses of the nodes connected by link. (Source: [18])

there are other peaks. These are at approximately 130, 250, and 400 km. The cause of these peaks seems to be that there are cities connected by *Shinkansen* (bullet train). Japan has well-developed transportation infrastructure; hence, cities at long distances can have many links. This indicates that geographic adjacency is not the exact direct facilitator of links; instead, it is the travel time required. If it takes a short time to travel between firms, they are likely to have links.

The intracity link ratio of a node in a specific city is defined as $r_k = k_{\text{inside}}/k$, where k is degree and k_{inside} is the number of links connected to nodes in the same city. The average link ratio, $\overline{r_k}$, is an average of r_k over all nodes in the same city

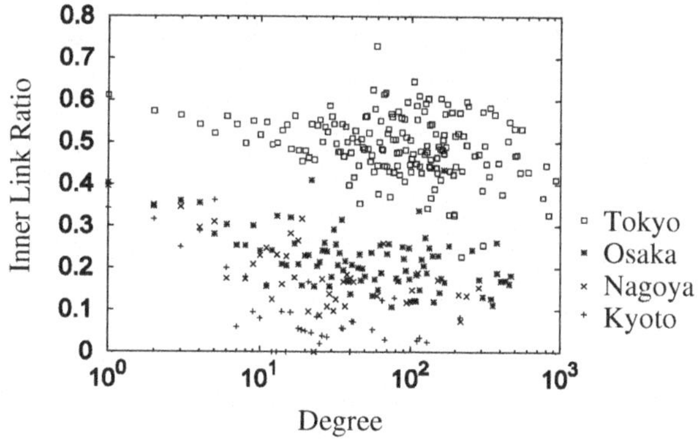

Fig. 2.7 Average link ratio, $\overline{r_k}$. (Source: [18])

with degree k. The four largest cities are addressed here. They are Tokyo's 23 special wards (a primary area of the capital), Osaka, Kyoto, and Nagoya. Figure 2.7 shows the average link ratio for all four cities. The horizontal axis indicates the degree k, and the vertical axis represents the average link ratio, $\overline{r_k}$.

There are negative correlations in all four cities. This means that a node with a small degree prefers to have links with nodes in the same region. However, a node with a large degree tends to have links with nodes in other regions.

2.3 Collaboration and Innovation

Effect of Team Size

We first illustrate the effect of team size on innovation. Previous studies have shown that inventor teams typically produce more successful patents than do solo inventors [31, 42]. However, it remains unknown whether firm teams will also outperform solo firms. The number of inventors or firms listed in a patent record is denoted m. An inventor or firm team is defined as having more than one listed inventor or firm in a patent record (i.e. $m \geq 2$). To quantify the innovation performance of inventors and firms, we define the impact (I) of a patent as the number of citations of that patent (with self-citations removed) normalized by the average number of citations of patents granted in the same year [14, 35]. We find that, on average, inventor teams outperform solo inventors (see Fig. 2.8a), which is consistent with previous results [42]. However, at the firm level, teams do not outperform solo inventors (see Fig. 2.8d). In fact, the average patent impact of US firm teams is even less than that of US solo firms. To further compare the performance of solo and team inventors, we separately calculate the impact distributions $P(I)$ of patents invented by solo and team inventors (Fig. 2.8b–f). The findings indicate that $P(I)$ displays fat-tailed distributions at both the inventor and firm levels, consistent with the result of $P(I)$ calculated for all patent records regardless of whether they were filed by inventors or firms.

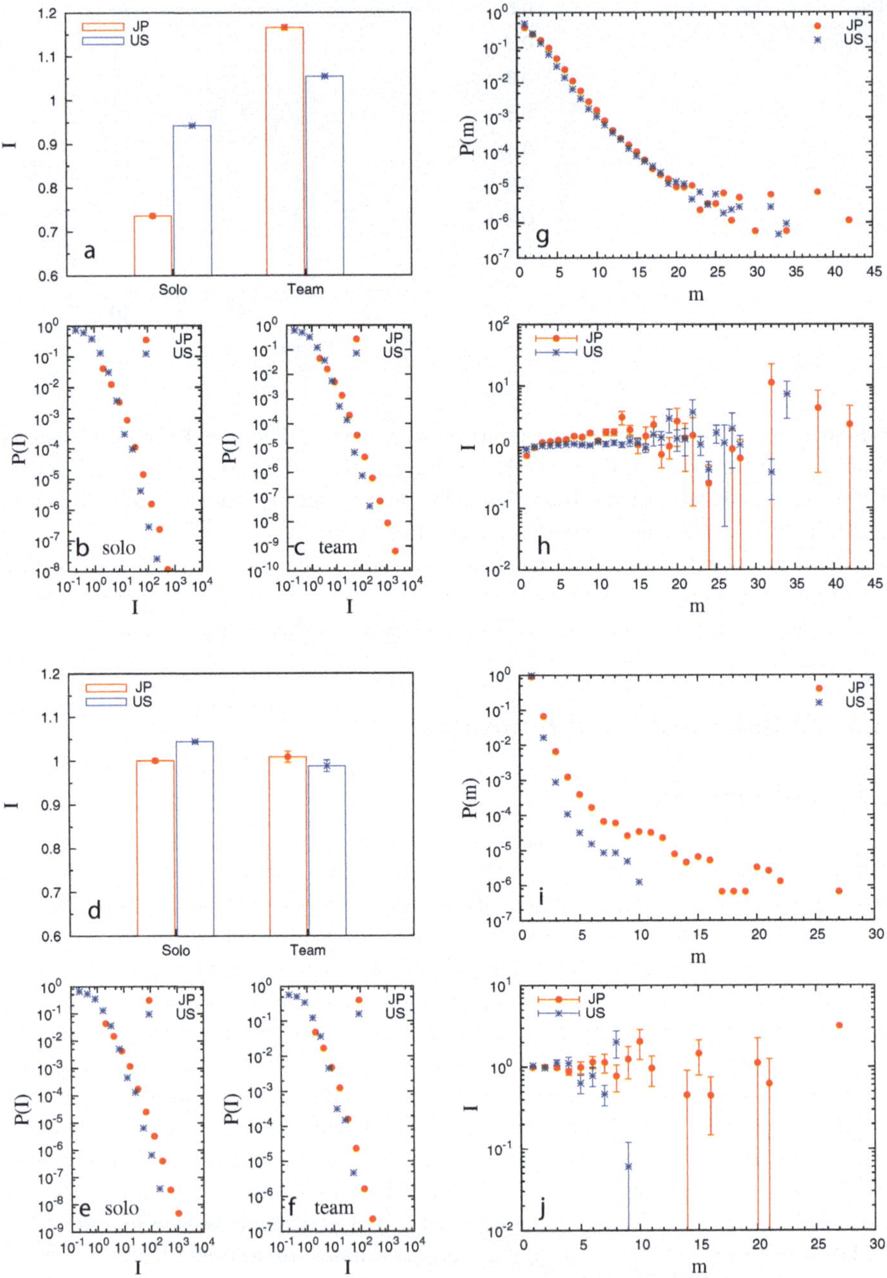

Fig. 2.8 Effect of team size on innovation performance. (**a**, **b**, **c**, **g**, **h**) Inventors. (**d**, **e**, **f**, **i**, **j**) Firms. (**a**, **d**) The average impacts of patents filed by solo and team inventors. (**b**, **c**, **e**, **f**) The impact distribution of patents filed by solo ($m = 1$) and team ($m \geq 2$) inventors. (**g**, **i**) The team size distribution. (**h**, **j**) Patent impact as a function of team size. (Source: [16])

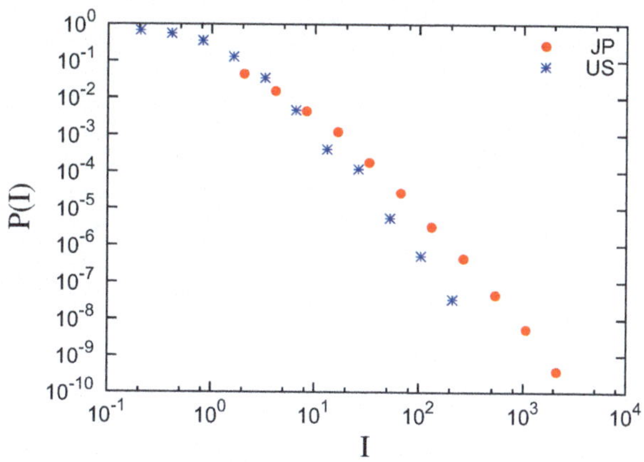

Fig. 2.9 Impact distributions of patents. Due to the logarithmic scale, the fraction of patents with zero impact value ($P(I = 0)$) is not shown: $P(I = 0) = 0.844$ for Japanese patents and 0.271 for US patents. (Source: [16])

Figure 2.9 shows the distribution of the impact. Both Japanese and US patents show highly heterogeneous impact distributions, implying that most patents have very low impact and that few patents have a substantial impact. This might be because patent applicants in the United States have a legal duty to cite any prior related patents, while in Japan, applicants had no such legal duty before 2002. Although the Japanese patent law was revised in 2002 to introduce a duty to disclose, the effect on the patent records studied in this work is rather small because 86.7% of patent citations occurred before 2002. Moreover, the impact values of Japanese patents have a broader distribution than that of US patents. These results indicate that Japanese patents have greater disparity in impact values than US patents.

To reveal more information about the effect of team size on innovation, we systematically study patent impact (I) as a function of team size (m) (Fig. 2.8h, j). Team performance, as measured by the impact of a team's patents, behaves differently at the two different levels as team size increases. For inventor teams, the patent impact increases slowly as team size m increases (up to $m \approx 15$), especially for Japanese inventor teams, which is consistent with the results shown in Fig. 2.8a. For firm teams, however, patent impact does not increase significantly in m, which is consistent with the results shown in Fig. 2.8d. Moreover, both inventor and firm teams exhibit substantial performance fluctuations as team size m becomes large, which could be because large teams are fairly rare in both Japanese and US patent records (see Fig. 2.8g, i).

Effect of Team Experience

Repeat Collaboration

Team experience is an important factor that could affect a team's innovation performance. To demonstrate the effect of team experience on innovation, one can

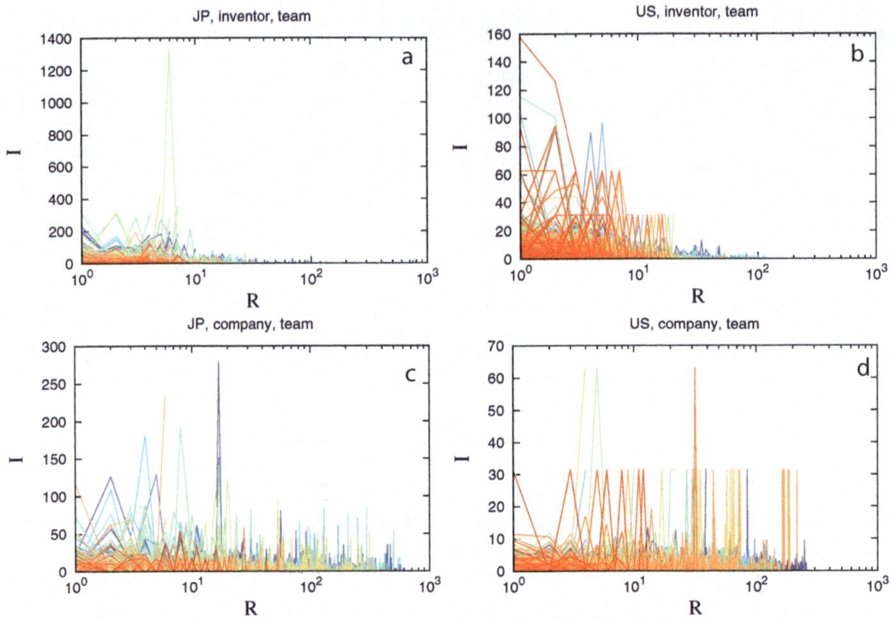

Fig. 2.10 Track records of individual teams with at least three patent records. Different colours represent different individual teams. (**a**, **b**) Inventors; (**c**, **d**) firms. (Source: [16])

simply track the performance of each team. For a given team, represented by a set of inventors or firms, its *exact repetition number* (R) is defined as the accumulated number of patent applications that the whole team has filed jointly up to the current patent. We then categorize teams into their inventor or firm set and track each team's performance by plotting the impact of its patents as a function of R (see Fig. 2.10). Extremely successful patents (indicated by their substantial impact) are typically among the first 10 patents of most inventor teams. For firm teams, the patent records exhibit many impact spikes, indicating that firm teams occasionally perform extremely well.

In the above analysis, we consider repeat collaborations of the whole team rather than its members. Before an entire team collaborates again, some of its members may have already collaborated or worked alone on other patents. To account for this and systematically study the effect of repeat collaboration on innovation using all the patent records of teams, R_{ij} of a node pair (i, j) in a patent record is denoted as the accumulated number of repeat collaborations between i and j up to that patent. Then, the *repeat collaboration number* (R_l) of a team listed in a patent record is defined as the average R_{ij} of all its teammate pairs. Note that for any given patent, the repeat collaboration number of the inventor team and that of the firm team are generally different. For example, in Fig. 2.1, for patent 2, $R_l = (1+1+2)/3 = 4/3$ for the inventor team, while $R_l = 1$ for the firm team.

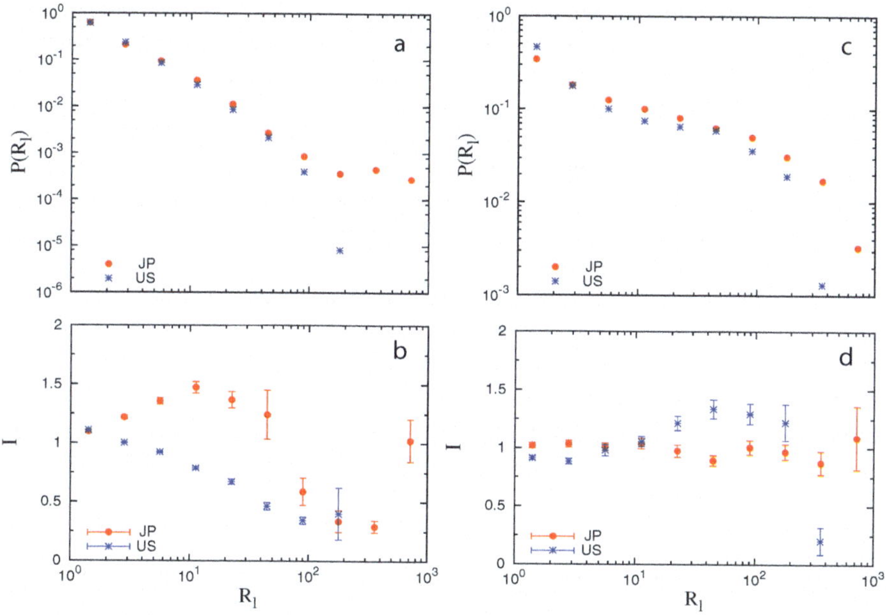

Fig. 2.11 Effect of repeat collaboration on innovation performance. (**a**, **b**) Inventors; (**c**, **d**) firms. (**a**, **c**) Probability distributions of the repeat collaboration numbers of teams. (**b**, **d**) Patent impact as a function of repeat collaboration numbers. (Source: [16])

For each patent in a team's record, we calculate its R_l and find that R_l shows a broad distribution for both inventor and firm teams (see Fig. 2.11a, c). We then calculate the average patent impact for teams with similar R_l grouped in logarithmic bins (see Fig. 2.11b, d). We find that the effects of repeat collaboration at the inventor and firm levels are qualitatively different. At the inventor level, Japanese teams and US teams also display notably different behaviour. The innovation performance of Japanese inventor teams first improves as R_l increases, reaches its peak value at $R_l = 10$, and then generally decreases for $R_l > 10$ (except for the abnormal behaviour around $R_l \approx 700$, where the patent impacts increase but are still not significantly higher than that of teams with $R_l < 10$.) This suggests an ideal timing for Japanese inventors to make new collaborations and hence "rejuvenate" the inventor team. In contrast, the performance of US inventor teams degrades almost monotonically as R_l increases, implying that repeat collaborations weakens the creativity of US inventor teams. At the firm level, Japanese teams show remarkably stable performance for R_l up to 10^3. For US firm teams, their performance improves slightly as R_l increases up to 100 and then decreases as R_l increases.

To quantify the innovation experience of a node, the productivity of a node i in a patent record is defined as the number of patents that node i has already contributed up to the current patent. Then, the *team productivity*, denoted R_n, of a team is the average of all its members' productivity. For example, in Fig. 2.1, the average productivity of the inventor team in patent 3 is $R_n = (1+2+3)/3 = 2$. Note that the repeat collaboration number (R_l) of a team quantifies the accumulated collaboration experience among its team members, which cannot be deduced from the average productivity of the team (R_n). For each patent in the records, we calculate the productivity of its inventor team or firm team. We find that at both the inventor and firm levels, productivity shows similar distributions for Japanese and US patents (see Fig. 2.12a, c). At the inventor level, $P(R_n)$ shows fat-tail behaviour, indicating that many patents are filed by unproductive inventors and only a few patents are filed by highly productive inventors. In contrast, at the firm level, $P(R_n)$ shows an almost uniform distribution for R_n up to 10^4, implying that firm teams with a wide range of productivity values contribute equally to innovations. The drastic decline in $P(R_n)$ as $R_n > 10^4$ for both Japanese and US firms suggests a natural upper bound of innovation productivity at the firm level. We then calculate the average impact of patents of similar productivity grouped in logarithmic bins (see Fig. 2.12b, d). At the inventor level, Japanese and US patents display clearly different behaviour. Japanese inventors' innovation performance first improves as R_n increases, reaches its peak value around $R_n \sim 40$, and then generally decreases. In contrast, the performance of US inventors decreases almost monotonically as R_n increases. At the firm level, both Japanese and US firms display relatively stable behaviour for productivity R_n up to 10^3. Note that repetitions of joint application by firm teams are probably

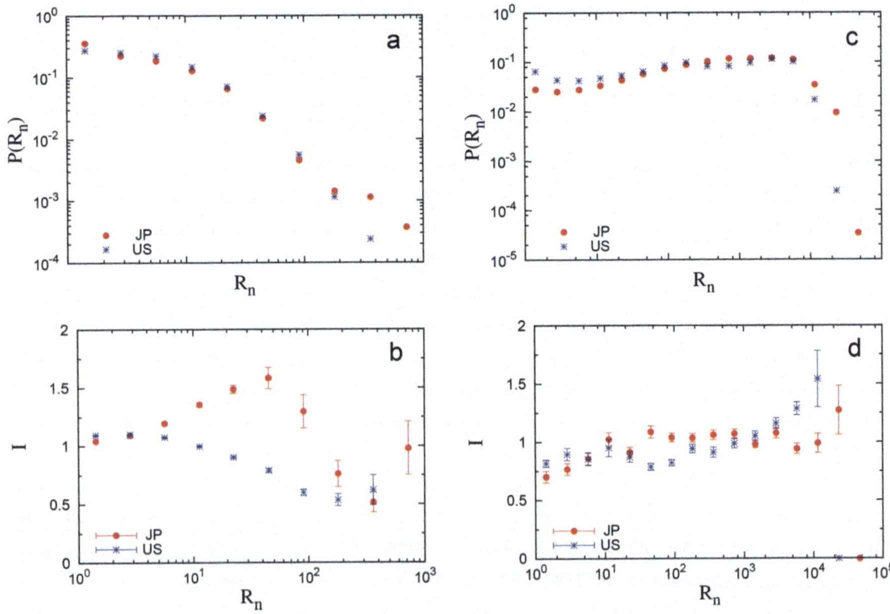

Fig. 2.12 Effects of team productivity on patent impact. (**a, b**) Inventors; (**c, d**) firms. (**a, c**) Probability distribution of team productivity. (**b, d**) Patent impact as a function of team productivity. (Source: [16])

conducted by different inventors. The stability of firm innovation performance across different inventors is subject to organizational influence. Furthermore, the innovation performance of US firms improves slightly as $R_{\mathrm{n}} > 10^3$ until a dramatic performance decrease is observed as $R_{\mathrm{n}} > 10^4$. Since the fraction of patents with $R_{\mathrm{n}} > 10^4$ is rather small ($\leq 0.01\%$), such degradation could be due to statistical noise.

Regression Analysis

In addition to the exact repetition number (R) and the repeat collaboration number (R_{l}) of a team, several variables are related to team experience, e.g. *team age* (denoted A, the average of the team members' "age", i.e. the time from the first application year to the current application year). (See Table 2.2.) The table reports variables related to team experience and other variables. To control for unobserved heterogeneity, we conduct a detailed regression analysis to investigate the effects of these team experience variables [31].

We also introduce a variable for an offset term, i.e. cited_count_average (the average number of citations of patents applied for in the same year as patent i) such that the response variable (cited_count, i.e. the number of citations patent i obtained) is closely related to the definition of a patent's impact. Longevity is also introduced as a control variable. We analysed the correlations between the variables and considered what regression analyses we can conduct (see Tables 2.3, 2.4, 2.5, and 2.6). We do not use breadth_of_search as a control variable because it strongly correlates with the variable patent_references. All of the explanatory variables are related to team experience, e.g. inventor_age (or firm_age), team_productivity.

We employ a generalized linear mixed model [38]:

$$\lambda_i = \exp\left[\beta_0 + \sum_k \beta_k x_{ki} + \log(\text{cited\_count\_average\_i}) + r_i\right] \tag{2.1}$$

where λ_i is the response variable, i.e. the citation count, β_0 is the intercept, β_k is the coefficient for the k-th variable, x_{ki} is the k-th variable for patent i, and r_i denotes random noise following a gamma distribution.

The results indicate that at the inventor level, all of the control variables have significant coefficients (see Tables 2.7 and 2.8) and the results are consistent with previous work [31]. For example, the control variable team_size is significant and has a positive coefficient for both Japanese and US inventors (consistent with the result depicted in Fig. 2.8a). At the firm level, some of the control variables do not have significant coefficients in some data sets (see Tables 2.9 and 2.10). For example, the control variable team_size of Japanese firms is not significant (consistent with the result depicted in Fig. 2.8d); the control variable longevity of Japanese firms is also not significant.

Table 2.2 Variables used in the regression analyses. (Source: [16])

Response variable	
Cited_count	Number of citations the patent received
Offset	
cited_count_average	Average number of citations of patents applied for in the same year as the current patent
Control variables	
patent_class	US patent class (in the United States) or IPC (in Japan)
team_size	Number of inventors/companies
Unassigned[a]	1 if the patent has no applicant
University[a]	1 if the patent has one or more universities as applicant
Claims	Number of claims
patent_references	Number of backward citations that the patent made to other patents
Longevity	Average of team member's duration (i.e. the time from application year to the last application year)
Explanatory variables related to team experience	
inventor_age (A)	Average of team member's "age" (i.e. the duration from its first application year
	to the application year of the current patents)
team_patents (R)	Number of patents for which the entire whole team has applied
team_experience_diversity	Number of technology classes (IPC sub-classes) to which the team has applied
team_network_size	Number of inventors/companies connected by two steps from inventors/companies
team_productivity (R_n)	Average number of patents that inventors/companies of a team have already applied for
repeat_collaboration_number (R_1)	Average number of repeat collaborations among teammate pairs

[a] can only be defined for inventors

Table 2.3 Correlation matrix of JP inventor. (Source: [16])

	(1)	(2)	(3)	(4)	(5)	(6)	(7)	(8)	(9)	(10)	(11)	(12)	(13)
(1) cited_count	1.00												
(2) team_size	0.02	1.00											
(3) unassigned	0.02	−0.02	1.00										
(4) university	−0.01	0.01	0.08	1.00									
(5) claims	0.01	0.08	0.22	0.02	1.00								
(6) patent_references	0.08	0.01	−0.03	−0.01	0.05	1.00							
(7) longevity	0.02	0.01	−0.27	−0.04	−0.03	0.10	1.00						
(8) inventor_age (A)	−0.04	0.00	−0.21	−0.02	0.06	0.07	0.75	1.00					
(9) team_patents (R)	0.00	0.15	−0.11	−0.02	0.05	0.08	0.49	0.48	1.00				
(10) team_experience_diversity	−0.01	0.23	−0.19	−0.02	0.00	0.02	0.54	0.55	0.60	1.00			
(11) team_network_size	0.00	0.28	−0.14	−0.02	0.08	0.08	0.48	0.54	0.55	0.62	1.00		
(12) team_productivity (R_n)	0.00	0.00	−0.10	−0.02	0.02	0.07	0.47	0.45	0.90	0.48	0.39	1.00	
(13) team_collaboration_number (R_1)	0.00	0.00	−0.05	−0.01	0.03	0.03	0.27	0.22	0.46	0.20	0.14	0.71	1.00

Table 2.4 Correlation matrix of US inventor. (Source: [16])

	(1)	(2)	(3)	(4)	(5)	(6)	(7)	(8)	(9)	(10)	(11)	(12)	(13)
(1) cited_count	1.00												
(2) team_size	−0.02	1.00											
(3) unassigned	0.01	−0.08	1.00										
(4) university	0.00	0.00	−0.04	1.00									
(5) claims	0.08	0.06	−0.03	0.05	1.00								
(6) patent_references	0.01	0.02	0.01	0.00	0.19	1.00							
(7) longevity	0.05	0.01	−0.14	−0.02	0.02	0.00	1.00						
(8) inventor_age (*A*)	−0.10	0.05	−0.11	−0.01	0.05	0.08	0.72	1.00					
(9) team_patents (*R*)	−0.06	0.19	−0.03	−0.02	0.02	0.04	0.39	0.45	1.00				
(10) team_experience_diversity	−0.04	0.18	−0.03	−0.02	0.02	0.05	0.42	0.49	0.77	1.00			
(11) team_network_size	−0.07	0.32	−0.08	−0.03	0.02	0.00	0.29	0.37	0.56	0.42	1.00		
(12) team_productivity (R_n)	−0.06	0.03	−0.02	−0.02	0.01	0.04	0.41	0.46	0.93	0.77	0.39	1.00	
(13) team_collaboration_number (R_1)	−0.05	0.03	−0.04	−0.01	0.01	0.07	0.32	0.33	0.45	0.25	0.19	0.58	1.00

Table 2.5 Correlation matrix of Japan firm. (Source: [16])

	(1)	(2)	(3)	(4)	(5)	(6)	(7)	(8)	(9)	(10)	(11)
(1) cited_count	1.00										
(2) team_size	−0.01	1.00									
(3) claims	0.01	0.00	1.00								
(4) patent_references	0.04	−0.01	0.07	1.00							
(5) longevity	−0.02	−0.06	0.07	0.05	1.00						
(6) company_age (A)	−0.07	−0.05	0.19	0.02	0.74	1.00					
(7) team_patents (R)	−0.03	0.06	0.13	−0.01	0.39	0.51	1.00				
(8) team_experience_diversity	−0.01	0.06	0.08	−0.02	0.57	0.60	0.73	1.00			
(9) team_network_size	−0.07	0.09	0.14	−0.04	0.44	0.64	0.61	0.78	1.00		
(10) team_productivity (R_n)	−0.03	−0.06	0.13	−0.02	0.41	0.53	0.96	0.74	0.61	1.00	
(11) team_collaboration_number (R_1)	−0.03	−0.04	0.06	−0.05	0.33	0.40	0.35	0.37	0.35	0.38	1.00

Table 2.6 Correlation matrix of US firm. (Source: [16])

	(1)	(2)	(3)	(4)	(5)	(6)	(7)	(8)	(9)	(10)	(11)
(1) cited_count	1.00										
(2) team_size	−0.01	1.00									
(3) claims	0.04	−0.03	1.00								
(4) patent_references	0.01	−0.01	0.15	1.00							
(5) longevity	0.08	−0.04	−0.02	−0.06	1.00						
(6) company_age (A)	−0.15	−0.02	0.09	0.03	0.69	1.00					
(7) team_patents (R)	−0.05	−0.01	0.12	0.03	0.33	0.52	1.00				
(8) team_experience_diversity	0.01	−0.02	0.08	0.00	0.52	0.62	0.84	1.00			
(9) team_network_size	−0.12	0.03	0.08	−0.01	0.27	0.54	0.77	0.76	1.00		
(10) team_productivity (R_n)	−0.05	−0.06	0.13	0.03	0.35	0.54	0.99	0.84	0.76	1.00	
(11) team_collaboration_number (R_1)	−0.04	0.21	0.00	−0.01	0.16	0.24	−0.05	−0.06	−0.05	0.00	1.00

Table 2.7 Regression result of Japan inventor. (Source: [16])

	(1)	(2)	(3)	(4)	(5)	(6)	(7)
team_size	3.73E-02 ***	3.54E-02 ***	3.75E-02 ***	3.58E-02 ***	3.67E-02 ***	3.73E-02 ***	3.73E-02 ***
unassinged	−6.672-02 ***	−1.06-01 ***	−6.71-02 ***	−6.52-02 ***	−6.70-02 ***	−6.66-02 ***	−6.61-02 ***
university	−6.11E-01 ***	−5.96E-01 ***	−6.11E-01 ***	−6.10E-01 ***	−6.10E-01 ***	−6.11E-01 ***	−6.12E-01 ***
claims	1.85E-02 ***	2.22E-02 ***	1.85E-02 ***	1.85E-02 ***	1.85E-02 ***	1.85E-02 ***	1.85E-02 ***
patent_references	6.98E-02 ***	7.16E-02 ***	6.98E-02 ***	6.98E-02 ***	6.97E-02 ***	6.98E-02 ***	6.97E-02 ***
longevity	1.34E-03 ***	5.36E-03 ***	1.36E-03 ***	1.23E-03 ***	1.30E-03 ***	1.44E-03 ***	1.44E-03 ***
inventor_age (A)		−9.95E-02 ***					
team_patents (R)			−6.14E-05				
team_experience_diversity				2.64E-03			
team_network_size					2.86E-05		
team_productivity (R_n)						−5.89E-04	
repeat_collaboration_number (R_1)							−2.03E-03 **
AIC	496,625	495,361	496,627	496,625	496,627	496,624	496,616

[a] $.p < 0.1$; $^{*}p < 0.05$; $^{**}p < 0.01$; $^{***}p < 0.001$

Model name: (1) base, (2) inventor_age (A), (3) team_patents, (4) team_experience_diversity, (5) team_network_size, (6) team_productivity (R_n), (7) repeat_collaboration_number (R_1)

Table 2.8 Regression result of US inventor. (Source: [16])

	(1)	(2)	(3)	(4)	(5)	(6)	(7)
team_size	6.32E-03 ***	1.10E-02 ***	1.67E-02 ***	1.36E-02 ***	2.13E-02 ***	7.43E-02 ***	6.61E-03 ***
unassinged	−4.86E-02 ***	−4.99E-02 ***	−3.34E-02 ***	−3.49E-02 ***	−4.87E-02 ***	−3.00E-02 ***	−4.35E-02 ***
university	1.02E-01 ***	1.05E-01 ***	9.31E-02 ***	1.01E-01 ***	9.16E-02 ***	9.38E-02 ***	9.58E-02 ***
claims	1.21E-02 ***	1.24E-02 ***	1.21E-02 ***	1.21E-02 ***	1.21E-02 ***	1.21E-02 ***	1.21E-02 ***
patent_references	5.70E-03 ***	7.65E-03 ***	6.09E-03 ***	5.97E-03 ***	5.78E-03 ***	6.13E-03 ***	6.21E-03 ***
longevity	9.70E-03 ***	3.98E-02 ***	1.61E-02 ***	1.46E-02 ***	1.34E-02 ***	1.67E-02 ***	1.48E-02 ***
inventor_age (A)		−7.14E-02 ***					
team_patents (R)			−4.08E-03 ***				
team_experience_diversity				1.24E-02 ***			
team_network_size					8.69E-04 ***		
team_productivity (R_n)						1.01E-02 ***	
repeat_collaboration_number (R_1)							−3.40E-02 ***
AIC	4,777,886	4,760,859	4,773,178	4,775,636	4,774,700	4,772,801	4,773,218

[a] . $p < 0.1$; * $p < 0.05$; ** $p < 0.01$; *** $p < 0.001$
Model name: (1) base, (2) inventor_age (A), (3) team_patents, (4) team_experience_diversity, (5) team_network_size, (6) team_productivity (R_n), (7)repeat_collaboration_number (R_1)

Table 2.9 Regression result of Japan firm. (Source: [16])

	(1)	(2)	(3)	(4)	(5)	(6)	(7)
team_size	−4.02E-02 .	−4.92E-02 *	−3.98E-02 .	−4.50E-02 *	−3.99E-02 .	−4.01E-02 .	−4.06E-02 .
claims	2.91E-02 ***	3.99E-02 ***	2.92E-02 ***	2.90E-02 ***	2.91E-02 ***	2.91E-02 ***	2.91E-02 ***
patent_references	6.73E-02 ***	6.45E-02 ***	6.72E-02 ***	6.80E-02 ***	6.72E-02 ***	6.74E-02 ***	6.56E-02 ***
longevity	−1.30E-03	4.20E-02 ***	−1.13E-03	−3.97E-03	1.14E-03	−1.48E-03	3.50E-04
inventor_age (A)		−8.71E-02 ***					
team_patents (R)			−5.97E-07				
team_experience_diversity				3.69E-04 *			
team_network_size					−1.56E-06 ***		
team_productivity (R_n)						1.25E-06	
repeat_collaboration_number (R_1)							−7.25E-04 **
AIC	55,714	55,431	55,716	55,712	55,716	55,716	55,708

[a] . $p<0.1$; * $p<0.05$; ** $p<0.01$; *** $p<0.001$
Model name: (1) base, (2) inventor_age (A), (3) team_patents, (4) team_experience_diversity, (5) team_network_size, (6) team_productivity (R_n), (7) repeat_collaboration_number (R_1)

Table 2.10 Regression result of US firm. (Source: [16])

	(1)	(2)	(3)	(4)	(5)	(6)	(7)
team_size	−4.87E-01 **	4.98E-02 **	2.73E-05 *	4.60E-02 **	4.24E-02 *	−5.93E-02 ***	3.15E-02 .
claims	1.55E-02 ***	1.60E-02 ***	4.33E-02 ***	1.42E-02 ***	1.49E-02 ***	1.38E-02 ***	1.55E-02 ***
patent_references	1.30E-02 ***	1.36E-02 ***	1.26E-02 ***	1.28E-02 ***	1.32E-02 ***	1.26E-02 ***	1.29E-02 ***
longevity	6.51E-03 ***	1.06E-02 ***	−1.94E-03 .	−1.59E-03	4.35E-03 ***	1.56E-03	6.02E-03 ***
inventor_age (A)		−7.25E-03 ***					
team_patents (R)			2.73E-05 ***				
team_experience_ diversity				1.38E-03 ***			
team_network_size					1.20E-04 ***		
team_productivity (R_n)						5.80E-05	
repeat_collaboration_ number (R_1)							1.49E-04 ***
AIC	126,666	126,642	126,461	126,448	126,585	126,448	126,656

[a] . $p<0.1$; * $p<0.05$; ** $p<0.01$; *** $p<0.001$
Model name: (1) base, (2) inventor_age (A), (3) team_patents, (4) team_experience_diversity, (5) team_network_size, (6) team_productivity (R_n), (7) repeat_collaboration_number (R_1)

One valuable application of the regression analyses is to compare the explanatory power of the explanatory variables. To do so, we assess the relative goodness of fit of seven statistical models that include different sets of variables:

(1) base model, which contains the following control variables: {team_size, unassigned, university, claims, patent_reference, and longevity}.
(2) base model + team_age (inventor_age or firm_age).
(3) base model + team_patents (R).
(4) base model + team_experience_diversity.
(5) base model + team_network_size.
(6) base model + team_productivity (R_{n}).
(7) base model + repeat_collaboration_number (R_{l}).

For each statistical model, we calculate the Akaike information criterion (AIC) value. A model with a lower AIC value means that it can fit the data better. We employ the differences in AIC values of the models to compare the team experience variables. The results indicate that the performance of the statistical models with different explanatory variables varies considerably, as their AIC values depend substantially on the data set (see the bottoms of Tables 2.7, 2.8, 2.9, and 2.10).[1] However, models (2) and (7) display relatively stable performance in the sense that they always have lower AIC values than the base model. This indicates that team_age (A) and repeat_collaboration_number (R_{l}) perform better than other explanatory variables in explaining the data sets.

Moreover, coefficients of A and R_{l} are negative for all data sets, except that the coefficient of R_{l} for the US firm data set is slightly positive. Note that the small positive coefficient of R_{l} for the US firm data set is consistent with the result depicted in Fig. 2.11d, where we observe that US firm teams' performance improves slightly as R_{l} increases up to 100 and then decreases as R_{l} increases further.

We also specifically assessed the control variables and one of the explanatory variables. Specifically, it is possible to simultaneously compare these variables using automatic variable selection algorithms, e.g. the least absolute shrinkage and selection operator (LASSO) method [34]. The LASSO results are shown in Table 2.11. The variables are ordered below according to their importance. The best models have minimum mean-squared errors. We found the following: (1) There are no decisive explanatory variables because their orderings were different when comparing the inventor (and firm) data sets. (2) A and R_{l} had relatively higher priorities than the other explanatory variables. (3) The Japanese inventor and firm data sets did not converge. However, the US inventor and firm data sets did converge, and A, R_{n}, and R_{l} were included in the converged models. Based on these findings, we argue that age (A) and repeat_collaboration_number (R_{l}) are certainly related to the impact of patents.

[1] Since each data set has a different number of observations, AIC values generally differ between data sets.

Table 2.11 Result of automatic variable selection by LASSO. (Source: [16])

Order	JP inventor	US inventor	JP company	US company
(1)	intercept	intercept	intercept	intercept
(2)	patents_references	claims	claims	claims
(3)	claims	patents_references	patents_references	team_experience_diversity
(4)	longevity	inventor_age (A)	company_age (A)	patents_references
(5)	team_size	team_collaboration_number (R_1)	team_experience_diversity	company_age (A)
(6)	team_network_size	team_productivity (R_n)	team_size	team_productivity (R_n)
(7)	inventor_age (A)	longevity	longevity	team_collaboration_number (R_1)
(8)	team_patents (R)	team_network_size	team_collaboration_number (R_1)	longevity
(9)	team_collaboration_number (R_1)	team_size	team_network_size	team_size
(10)	university	university	team_patents (R)	team_network_size
(11)	team_experience_diversity	team_patents (R)	team_productivity (R_n)	team_patents (R)
(12)	team_productivity (R_n)	unssigned		
(13)	unssigned	team_experience_diversity		

Explanatory variables related to team experience Grayout cells mean variables were not included into an optimal model

Interplay Between Team Age and Repeat Collaboration

The result of the regression analysis prompts us to study the interplay between A and R_{I}, i.e. the "ageing" of team members and the repeat collaborations among them. Naturally the degradation of team performance with large R_{I} could be because teams become less innovative as they become older (i.e. A is very large). (Actually, A shows similar features to R_{I}.) To address this issue and further reveal the intricate effect of collaboration on innovation, we group patents into quartiles by team age, and then for each group, we calculate the patent impact as a function of R_{I} (see Fig. 2.13). Now, within each group, the change in innovation performance is due primarily to the repeat collaborations quantified by R_{I}. At the inventor level, for Japanese inventor teams, regardless of their team age, performance first improves as R_{I} increases and then decreases. US inventor teams' performance degrades almost monotonically with increasing R_{I}, regardless of team age. At the firm level, Japanese firm teams with different team ages show remarkably stable innovation performance as R_{I} increases. In contrast, US firm teams' performance displays highly unstable behaviour, and there is no significant improvement for large R_{I}, regardless of team age.

We have already defined *team age*, denoted A, by averaging the team members' "ages". Note that team age is not necessarily related to collaboration, as a very old team could simply be due to its team members being very old but not very productive and/or collaborative. For each patent in the records, we calculate the age of its inventor team and firm team. At the inventor level, $P(A)$ is highly heterogeneous, implying that most patents are invented by "young" inventors with small A, while only a few patents are invented by "old" inventors with large A. In contrast, at the firm level, $P(A)$ shows two strong peaks: (1) $A = 0$ for both US and Japanese teams and (2) $A \approx 8$ for Japanese teams or $A \approx 13$ for US teams. Japanese inventor teams and US inventor teams have roughly the same age distribution (see Fig. 2.14a). However, US firm teams and Japanese firm teams have notably different age distributions (see Fig. 2.14). We then calculate the average impact of patents of the same age (see Fig. 2.14b, d) and find that the team performance behaves differently at the two different levels as team age increases. At the inventor level, both Japanese and US inventor teams' performance gradually declines as team age A increases. A similar trend is observed for Japanese firm teams. However, US firm teams show very stable performance as A increases. Note that the performance of both inventor and firm teams with very high A displays substantial fluctuations, which could be because "old" teams are very rare in both the Japanese and US patent records (see Fig. 2.14a, c).

2.4 Discussion

Although a moderate level of repeat collaboration slightly improves the performance of Japanese inventor teams and US firm teams, we do not find any strong positive relationship between innovation and collaboration in the long run. The results

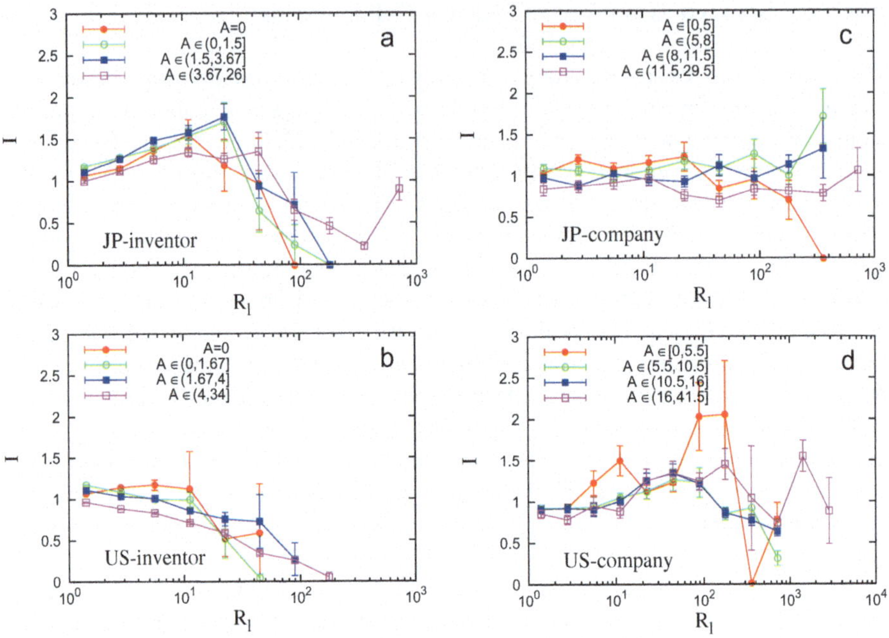

Fig. 2.13 Effect of repeat collaboration on innovation performance of teams with similar team age. (**a**,**b**) Inventors; (**c**,**d**) firms. To separate the ageing effect of a team from that of repeat collaboration among its teammates, we group patents according to the quartiles team age (A). The A range of each group is shown in the legend. For each A group, we further group patents according to their repeat collaboration number (R_l) and then calculate the average patent impact for each R_l subgroup. (Source: [16])

suggest that there is a negative relationship between them, especially at the inventor level and for long-term collaboration.

At the inventor level, Japanese inventor teams have a performance peak around repeat collaboration number $R_l \approx 10$, while the innovation performance of US inventor teams declines almost monotonically as R_l increases. This result raises an interesting question worthy of future study: What explains the drastically different effects of repeat collaboration on the performance of the two countries' inventor teams? We leave the systematic study of this question to future work. However, it is important to note the different innovation climates in the United States and Japan, which might help us to better understand this question. Typically, US workers are subject to strong pressure/incentives for immediate results and light labour market regulations [4], implying that for US inventors, taking time to deepen their collaborations is not a good strategy. In contrast, the Japanese labour market is subject to strict regulation, and a group of individuals can create joint value due to the country's cohesive corporate culture [28].

At the firm level, Japanese firm teams display remarkably stable innovation performance, while US firm teams slightly outperform on repeat collaborations up

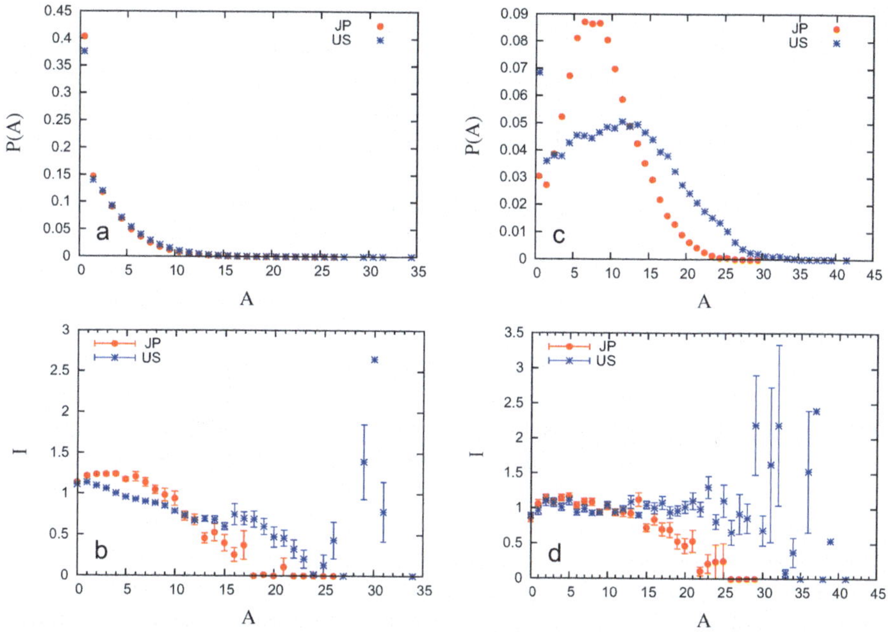

Fig. 2.14 Effects of team age on patent impact. (**a**, **b**) Inventors; (**c**,**d**) firms. (**a**, **c**) Probability distribution of team age. (**b**, **d**) Patent impact as a function of team age. (Source: [16])

to a certain point. This might be related to the fact that in the United States, joint patents by firms are not very common, while in Japan, joint patents between firms are widespread. This topic deserves a systematic study in the future. Note further that the difference in inter-firm relationships between the two countries could be useful to explain the observation. In Japan, there is a unique type of firm ties called "Keiretsu", i.e. a set of firms with interlocking business relationships and shareholdings and hence that typically share human assets and information [7]. Since "Keiretsu" substantially reduces the inter-firm/intra-firm distinction, there may be no margin to deepen these firms' collaborations on innovation. In contrast, US firms do not have such prior connections and hence could build deeper collaborations as they create more joint patents. Consequently, a longitudinal relationship between US firms nurtures trust and thus improves performance [43]. However, in the long run, overembeddedness limits the diversity of information and hence stifles creation [36]. This may explain the non-monotonic behaviour of the innovation performance of US firm teams.

The results presented here provide a novel perspective on strategy for improving innovation performance via controlling the repeat collaboration number at the inventor and/or firm levels. For example, our results suggest that repeat collaborations between Japanese firms exhibit highly stable performance, while repeat collaborations between Japanese inventors have a non-monotonic effect on their performance. Hence, Japanese firms should carefully monitor the repeat collaboration number

(R_I) of their inventor teams (rather than that of their firm teams) and force the inventors to develop new collaborations when R_I approaches 10. On the other hand, US inventor teams' performance degrades monotonically in the number of repeat collaborations, while US firm teams' performance peaks around $R_I \approx 100$. Hence, US firms should proactively collaborate with other firms but change the individuals involved in the inter-firm collaborations.

We expect that similar strategies could also be useful in other countries with similar innovation climates. Of course, quantitative studies of patent records from other countries need to be performed to address this open but interesting question. Particular care should be taken with respect to seemingly crucial factors such as non-structured social factors. In particular, to understand the impact of collaboration on innovations, it is necessary to recognize that different countries have different firm climates. For example, Japan and the United States have antithetical firm climates. The Japanese government regards large firms as important. The Japanese government promoted indirect financial systems after the Second World War, and Japanese banks financed large firms so that they could catch up on US technologies. By contrast, the US government strongly supports start-up firms. For example, there is a successful policy called Small Business Innovations Research (SBIR) that consists of three phases, and only successful start-up firms can proceed to the next phase. The policy is the largest innovation policy in the United States [41]. Based on the above discussion, when the systematic approach proposed in this chapter is applied to different data sets obtained from different countries, it is necessary to first recognize the different firm climates in those countries so that we can better understand the impact of collaboration on innovation. We cannot blindly adopt strategies from other countries. In fact, Japan failed to introduce SBIR to the country at the first attempt [17].

Our systematic approach based on team size and repeat collaboration may also be readily applied to other creative projects, such as scientific research [13, 25], consulting practice [29], and entertainment performances [6, 13, 24, 37], to further reveal the intricate relation between collaboration and creativity.

References

1. http://www.japio.or.jp/english/
2. http://www.nber.org/
3. Barabási AL, Oltvai ZN. Network biology: understanding the cell's functional organization. Nat Rev Genet. 2004;5:101–13.
4. Bloom N, Reenen JV. Why do management practices differ across firms and countries? J Econ Perspect. 2010;24(1):203–24.
5. Chesbrough HW. Open innovation. Boston: Harvard Business School; 2003.
6. Delmestri G, Montanari F, Usai A. Reputation and strength of ties in predicting commercial success and artistic merit of independents in the Italian feature film industry*. J Manag Stud. 2005;42(5):975–1002.
7. Dyer JH. Does governance matter? Keiretsu alliances and asset specificity as sources of Japanese competitive acdvantage. Organ Sci. 1996;7(6):649–67.

8. Fleming L, Marx M. Managing creativity in small worlds. Calif Manag Rev. 2006;48:6–27.
9. Fleming L, Sorenson O. Technology as a complex adaptive system: evidence from patent data. Res Policy. 2001;30:1019–39.
10. Fleming L, Mingo S, Chen D. Collaborative brokerage, generative creativity, and creative success. Admin Sci Q. 2007;52:443–75.
11. Grant RM. Toward a knowledge-based theory of the firm. Strateg Manag J. 1996;17:109–22.
12. Griliches Z. R&D and productivity-the economic evidence. Chicago: The University of Chicago Press; 1998.
13. Guimera R, et al. Team assembly mechanisms determine collaboration network structure and team performance. Science 2005;308(5722):697–702.
14. Hall BH, Jaffe AB. The NBER patent citations data file: lessons, insights and methodological tools. National Bureau of Economic Research Working Paper 8498; 2000.
15. Hicks D, et al. Research excellence and patented innovation. Sci Public Policy. 2000;27(5):310–20.
16. Inoue H, Liu Y. Revealing the intricate effect of collaboration on innovation. PLoS ONE 2015;10(3):e0121973.
17. Inoue H, Yamaguchi E. Evaluation of the small business innovation research program in Japan. SAGE Open. 2017;7(1):1–9.
18. Inoue H, Souma W, Tamada S. Spatial characteristics of joint application networks in Japanese patents. Phys A. 2007;383:152–7.
19. Lai R, D'Amour A, Yu A, Sun Y, Fleming L. Disambiguation and Co-authorship Networks of the U.S. Patent Inventor Database (1975–2010); 2011.
20. Laursen K, Salter A. Open for innovation: the role of openness in explaining innovation performance among U.K. manufacturing firms. Strateg Manag J. 2006;27(2):131–50.
21. Newman MEJ. Assortative mixing in networks. Phys Rev Lett. 2002;89(20):208701.
22. Nonaka I, Lewin AY. A dynamic theory of organizational knowledge creation. Org Sci. 1994;5(1):14–37.
23. Pastor-Satorras R, Vázques A, Vespignani A. Dynamical and correlation properties of the internet. Phys Rev Lett. 2001;87(25):258701.
24. Perretti F, Negro G. Mixing genres and matching people: a study in innovation and team composition in Hollywood. J Organ Behav. 2007;586:563–86.
25. Porac JF, et al. Human capital heterogeneity collaborative relationships, and publication patterns in a multidisciplinary scientific alliance: a comparative case study of two scientific teams. Res Policy. 2004;33(4):661–678. ISSN: 0048-7333. https://doi.org/10.1016/j.respol.2004.01.007.
26. Porter ME. On competition. Boston: Harvard Business School Press; 1998.
27. Powell WW, Grodal S. The oxford handbook of innovation, chap. 3. Oxford: Oxford University Press; 2006, p. 56–85.
28. Ralston DA, et al. The impact of national culture and economic ideology on managerial work values: a study of the United States, Russia, Japan, and China. J Int Bus Stud. 2007;1–19.
29. Reagans R, Zuckerman E, McEvily B. How to make the team: social networks vs. demography as criteria for designing effective teams. Admin Sci Q. 2004;49(1):101–33.
30. Simonton DK. Scientific genius: a psychology of science. Cambridge: Cambridge University Press; 1988.
31. Singh J, Fleming L. Lone inventors as sources of technological break-throughs: myth or reality? Manag Sci. 2010;56:41–56.
32. Skilton PF, Dooley KJ. The effects of repeat collaboration on creative abrasion. Acad Manag Rev. 2010;35(1):118–34. ISSN: 0363-7425. https://doi.org/10.5465/AMR.2010.45577886.
33. Tamada S, Kodama F, Gemba K. A study on science linkage of Japanese patents; an analysis on patents in the field of genetic technology by constructing a citation database. J Sci Policy Res Manag. 2002;17(3/4):222–30.
34. Tibshirani R. Regression shrinkage and selection via the lasso. J R Stat Soc Ser B Methodol. 1996;58:267–288.

35. Trajtenberg M. A penny for your quotes: patent citations and the value of innovations. Rand J Econ. 1990;21(1):172–87.
36. Uzzi B. Social structure and competition in interfirm networks: the paradox of embeddedness. Admin Sci Q. 1997;42(1):35–67.
37. Uzzi B, Spiro J. Collaboration and creativity: the small world problem. Am J Sociol. 2005;111(2):447–504.
38. Venables WN, Ripley BD. Modern applied statistics with S. New York: Springer; 2002.
39. Watts DJ, Strogatz SH. Collective dynamics of 'small-world' networks. Nature. 1998;393:440–2.
40. Weisberg RW. Creativity: understanding innovation in problem solving, science, invention, and the arts. Hoboken: Wiley; 2006.
41. Wessner CW, editor. An assessment of the SBIR program. Washington, DC: National Academies Press; 2008.
42. Wuchty S, Jones BF, Uzzi B. The increasing dominance of teams in production of knowledge. Science. 2007;316(5827):1036–9.
43. Zaheer A, Mcevily B, Perrone V. Does of trust matter? Exploring the effects interorganizational and interpersonal trust on performance. Org Sci. 1998;9(2):141–59.

Chapter 3
The Innovator'S Dilemma in Collaboration

3.1 Introduction

Chapter 2 showed how the quality of collaborations changes when they are repeated. This chapter further investigates this issue, mainly with respect to the optimal time to maintain collaborations and the optimal time to switch to other collaborations. The findings in this chapter mainly rely on the author's prior work [10]. Most text, figures, and tables have been reproduced under the Creative Commons Attribution License. The main text is modified to fit the context of this book.

In Chap. 2, we illustrated the basic features of collaborations among inventors and firms. As previously discussed, recent studies have highlighted the importance of collaborations and have indicated that teams can generate better outcomes than solo researchers on average [24] and have also revealed a trend towards teams rather than solo researchers [13, 17, 24]. If teams perform better, the next question is what qualities of teams affect performance.

Repeat collaborations represent a good context to study team activities because we can observe the process of coordination in teams through repeat collaborations. There is also a growing literature on repeat collaborations that occur in creative projects. For example, Skilton and Dooley report that there is a sequence of processes consisting of idea generation, disclosure/advocacy, and convergence, which they call "creative abrasion" [22].

A review of the studies on repeat collaborations reveals that the repeat collaborations have two contradictory aspects. One aspect is positive: team development or experience. Studies of team development using various models have described the kinds of processes that allow team members to cultivate mutual relationships and improve performance [15, 21]. These studies have described the processes through which team members have cultivated mutual relationships and improved performance. The other aspect is negative: team degeneration or decline. Previous

H. Inoue, *Co-patenting: An Analytic Tool for Cooperative Research and Development*, Evolutionary Economics and Social Complexity Science 21,
https://doi.org/10.1007/978-4-431-54807-2_3

studies have found that repeat collaborations underperform initial collaborations in creative projects, e.g. scientific research [8, 11, 19], consulting practice [20], and performances in entertainment [2, 8, 18, 23].

Repeat collaborations are particularly discussed in psychology. The terms "habitual routines" or "behaviour of groups" refer to repeat collaborations. The first review of habitual routines of groups is to the best of our knowledge Gersick and Hackman [3], although they note that their paper does not provide either a literature review or a theory of habitual behaviour but rather presented a broad brush survey. They note that "habitual routines can reduce the likelihood of innovative performance processes".

This contradiction is not merely a theoretical conflict, and there is considerable empirical evidence on the topic. The contradiction is descriptively discussed with respect to innovation in firms in "The Innovator's Dilemma" [1]. This book, which contains numerous observed examples, explains how new companies with disruptive technologies redefine competitiveness in markets and that successful and preexisting companies have difficulty adjusting to changes because of past successes. Firms with successful products fixate their successes and are thus ultimately ruined. Although that author addresses the dilemma faced by individuals rather than firms, the dilemma that firms confront has the same basis.

In this chapter, the empirical findings are gleaned from extensive quantitative analyses of repeat collaborations on patent applications using data from Japan and the United States. In particular, the dilemma is defined as the phenomenon whereby a successful team is fixated on repeat collaborations even if performance declines and members of the team forgo the potential for achieving greater success on different teams. There are no existing quantitative analyses of this dilemma in the context of creative projects.

The psychological studies on the topic, at their core, attempt to reveal the mechanisms driving repeat collaborations. However, they intentionally avoid discussing the mechanisms themselves because there are no detailed data such as on communication in teams. Additionally, the difference between these psychological studies and the present work is attributable to the data employed. Their data are detailed but basically at the lab scale. In comparison, the data in this chapter are longitudinal and broad in scope. This means that the results of those studies and the present work complement one another.

By their nature, teams have routines because routines enable them to exploit the knowledge and coordination within teams and avoid unnecessary costs in reproducing such knowledge or coordination. Therefore, how teams can avoid the gradual performance decline while employing routines is a practical issue. Obviously, some stimuli are necessary to avoid gradual failure. Here, introducing individuals from new technological fields into teams and mixing team memberships are considered the stimuli, and data are used to investigate the effect of these stimuli. In particular, mixing team memberships has already been studied in psychology [4, 5].

3.2 Data

Patent data are suitable for studying creative projects. This is because patents indicate the occurrence of innovations over time [7]. Additionally, they contain a massive amount of information on repeat collaborations. We use the Institute of Intellectual Property (IIP) patent database to obtain the Japanese patent data [6] and the National Bureau of Economic Research (NBER) US patent citations data and Patent Network Dataverse to obtain the US patent data [9, 16]. Patent data are also published by the European Patent Office, called "PATSTAT". However, PATSTAT is not used because inventors are not identified, and considerable work is required to address it.

We can extract data with the same format and can thus compare the two databases. The data include the IDs of inventors who applied for patents, the number of received citations, the technological classifications of patents, and the year of application. This chapter uses the International Patent Class for Japanese patent data and the US patent class for US patent data to obtain the technological classifications. We use the number of citations to quantify patent performance [9]. Since older patents have more opportunities to be cited, we measure impact as the number of citations divided by the average number of citations of patents granted in the same year.

Here, teams are defined as groups of more than one individual. A team is uniquely identified by all participants. Therefore, even if all members of a team are members of other teams, the former team is distinguished from other teams that include all members of the former team. For example, if there is a sequence of patents where patent 1 is filed by inventors A and B and patent 2 is filed by inventors A, B, and C, we count two distinct first patents for the team of A and B and the team of A, B, and C. Although the team of A and B is a subset of the team of A, B, and C, they are considered two different teams. One might argue that the prior collaboration between inventors A and B means that patent 2 is not a first patent and, therefore, that it is not appropriate to count them as in a different team. This viewpoint might be correct. On the other hand, it is doubtful that these two collaborations (one with and one without inventor C) represent the same team. Therefore, a collaboration is counted when the set of inventors is identical. We revisit this issue in a later section and redefine how teams are counted.

Table 3.1 summarizes the basic data, which show that there are sufficient patents and cross-patent citations to apply statistical analysis to the problem at hand. We consider the longest time frame available in the data because longitudinal observation is necessary for this analysis.

Since the impact of team inventions is the central topic, we examine their distributions. Figure 3.1 plots the complementary cumulative probability distributions of team size in the data. The vertical axis represents the cumulative probability. The horizontal axis represents team size. The red plots are for Japanese data, and the blue plots are for US data. The lines are fitted to log-normal distributions using maximum

Table 3.1 Overview of data sets. Data sets used are Japanese (JP) and US patent data. The range of years in which patents were applied for is labeled "duration". In addition, table lists the numbers of patents, inventors, teams, and citations. (Source: [10])

Data sets	JP	US
Duration (year)	1964–2012	1975–2010
No. of patents	4,349,161	3,984,771
No. of inventors	1,538,525	2,665,7091
No. of teams	967,159	1,325,869
No. of citations	18,410,996	48,911,485

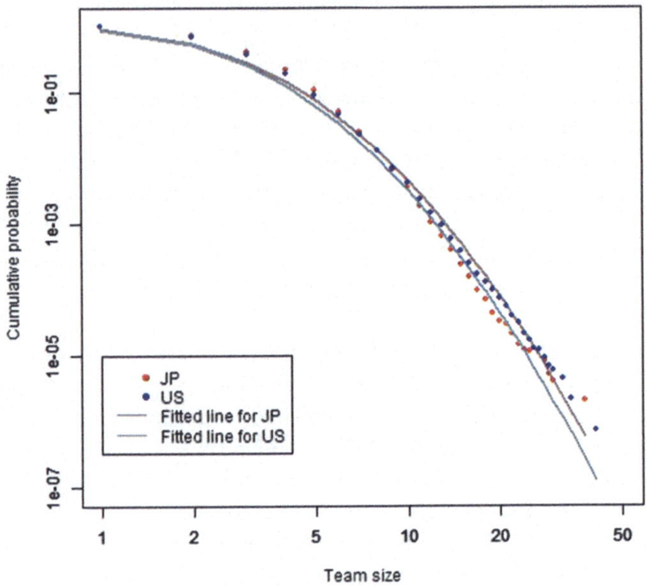

Fig. 3.1 Complementary cumulative probability distribution of team size. The horizontal axis shows team size. The vertical axis shows the cumulative probability. Lines are fitted to log-normal distributions. (Source: [10])

likelihood estimation. The greyish-red line is for Japan, and the greyish-blue line is for the United States. The lines seem to fit well to the plots.

Figures 3.2 and 3.3 depict the cumulative distributions of team size in the first and second halves of the covered time periods for the Japanese and US data, respectively. The interpretations of these figures are the same as that of Fig. 3.1. We observe that team sizes are growing in both countries. The result is in line with results of previous studies [8, 24].

Figure 3.4 plots the impact distributions for the data sets. The interpretations of the plots and fitted lines are the same as those in Fig. 3.1. Note that there are no considerable differences between data sets despite the different patent laws in the two countries. Regarding the fitted lines, the US distribution is well fitted by a log-normal distribution. In comparison, the Japanese distribution is not fitted as well as

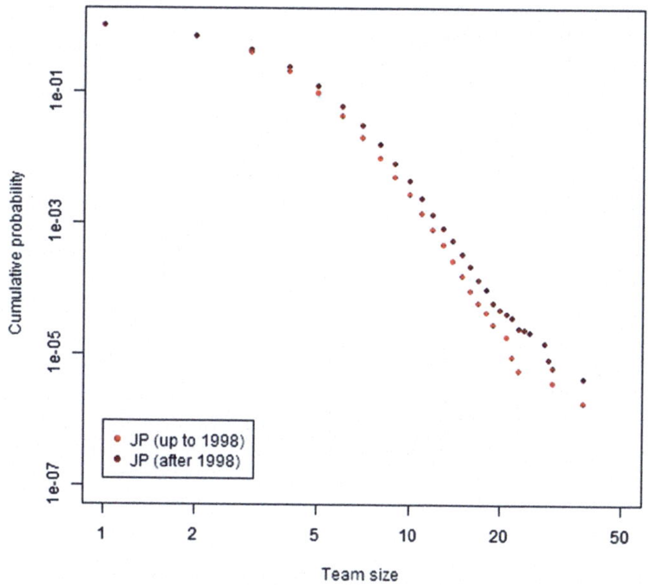

Fig. 3.2 Complementary cumulative probability distribution of team size in Japan. The horizontal axis shows team size. The vertical axis shows the cumulative probability. Data are separated around the middle of duration. (Source: [10])

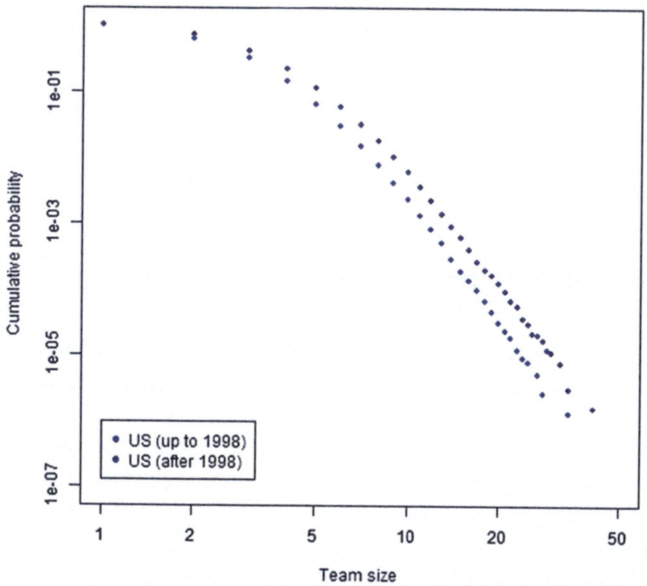

Fig. 3.3 Complementary cumulative probability distribution of team size in the United States. The horizontal axis shows team size. The vertical axis shows the cumulative probability. Data are separated around middle of duration. (Source: [10])

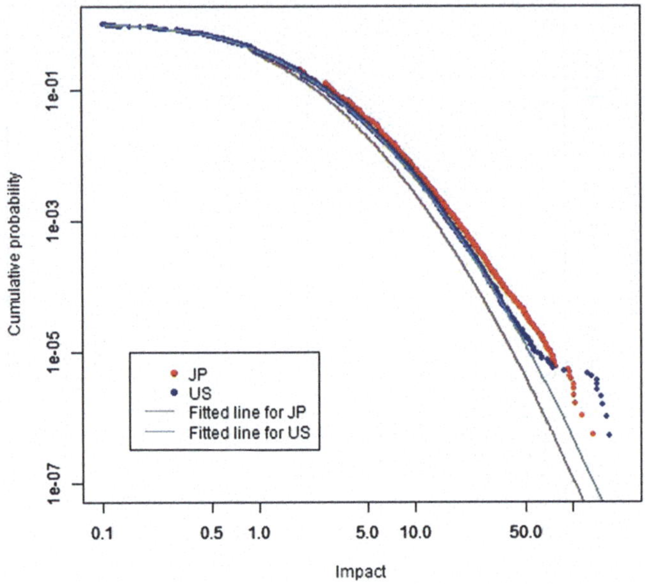

Fig. 3.4 Complementary cumulative probability distribution of impact. The horizontal axis shows the impact. The vertical axis shows the cumulative probability. Lines are fitted to log-normal distributions. (Source: [10])

the US distribution. Since an impact that is less than one is not frequently observed in Japan, this appears to be responsible for the deviation of the fitted line for Japan. A detailed investigation of the cause of this devision is beyond the scope of this work, but note that this difference could be explained by the difference in citation dynamics, which depend on national cultures.

3.3 Quantitative Demonstration of the Dilemma

Again, one of the goals in this chapter is to provide extensive quantitative analyses of the dilemma involved in collaboration on creative activities. We first describe the dilemma in the context of creative activities.

A typical example of the dilemma is that a successful team tends to attempt to reproduce past successes, while team members forgo opportunities to achieve other successes on different teams. Here, we propose three predictions to validate the dilemma.

- Prediction 1: The greater the impact that the patent that a team creates is, the longer the team will collaborate.
- Prediction 2: The impact of consecutive patents decreases after a team creates great patents (hits).

- Prediction 3: At some point while collaborating on consecutive patents, the expected impact of switching teams will exceed that from continuing with the same team.

Prediction 1 means that a team's creating a significant patent (hit) tends to bind members together for a long time. Teams attempt to reproduce past success if they succeed, while they will not continue together if they have been unsuccessful. Prediction 2 has already been reported in previous studies [8, 11]. The opposite of Prediction 2 is that there is no decrease or, instead, an increase in impact after creating hits. Prediction 3 means that individuals on teams with past successes forgo opportunities to produce better patents by switching teams. If all of these three predictions are supported by the data, we say that the dilemma exists.

Figure 3.5 plots the average number of patents made by a team after it creates a patent of a given impact. The impact of the first patent (the baseline patent) is shown on the horizontal axis, while the vertical axis represents the average number of subsequent patents by the same team. This average includes only the subsequent patents, not the baseline patent. Note that every patent by a team is used once as a baseline and the numbers of subsequent patents for all baseline patents are counted. This means that there are double or more counts of given patents.

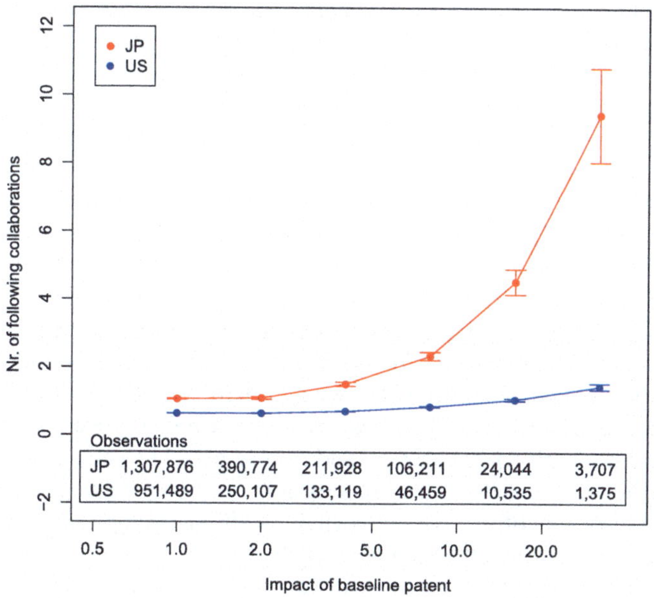

Fig. 3.5 Average number of patents made by a team after it completes a patent with a given impact. The horizontal axis is the impact of the baseline patent. The vertical axis is the average number of subsequent patents by the same team. Standard errors are in brackets. The horizontal axis is scaled such that the number of observations is greater than approximately 100. (Source: [10])

Linear regression analyses are conducted to determine whether the greater the impact of a team's patent is, the more subsequent patents that the team will produce. Although the relationships in Fig. 3.5 do not appear to be linear, as long as we obtain significantly positive results in the linear regression analyses, the results will be satisfactory. Both data sets have positive and significant coefficients for impact (Japan: coefficient $= 0.0042$, $p < 10^{-16}$; United States: coefficient $= 0.032$, $p < 10^{-16}$). Therefore, the greater the impact of a patent is, the more subsequent patents the teams will have. The results satisfy Prediction 1.

As the curves in Fig. 3.5 are concave, the probability of repeating a collaboration increases as the impact of a baseline patent increases. In addition, the more concave the curve, the more sensitive the response is. Therefore, Japanese teams' patents tend to have more subsequent patents, and the number is more sensitive to prior impacts than that for the US patents. To statistically test whether Japanese inventors have more subsequent patents than US inventors, we conduct Wilcoxon rank-sum tests. We selected this test because the distributions of subsequent patents do not resemble a normal distribution. The test is one-sided. For each impact bin in Fig. 3.5, we find that subsequent Japanese patents are dominant at the five-percent significance level.

Figure 3.6 plots the average impact of subsequent patents after hits. Here, hits are defined as patents in the top 10% of impact. The vertical axis is the average impact. The horizontal axis shows a patent's place in the sequence that includes the hit and subsequent patents. The red line is for Japan, and the blue line is for the United States. Those lines show repeat collaborations by teams whose membership did not change ("no switch"). As an overview of these results, teams that made hits in the past tend to subsequently create beneficial patents because the lines in Fig. 3.6 are above one, namely, the average impact. Since we observe a decline in repeat collaborations without switching teams, the data fulfil Prediction 2.

The greyish lines in Fig. 3.6 show the average impact of the first patents applied for by a new team. The greyish-red line is for Japan, and the greyish-blue line is for the United States ("switch to new team"). The new team includes individuals who belonged to teams that made hits. Since only the first patents with new teams are considered, repeat collaborations for "switch to new team" given on the horizontal axis have a different meaning from "no switch". Here, it is necessary to compare the difference between "no switch" and "switch to new team". If a member belonged to a team (with a hit) until repetition $r - 1$ and then switched to a new team, the impact of the first patent of the new team is plotted at r. By doing so, we can compare the average impact of repetition r of "no switch" with the average impact of the first patent of the team to which the member switched.

Comparing the lines between no switching and switching enables us to understand when individuals should switch teams. Wilcoxon rank-sum tests are conducted between no switching and switching to identify when the average impacts of switching significantly dominate not switching. As mentioned above, we select the Wilcoxon rank-sum test because the impact distribution is highly skewed. The test is one-sided. We find that switching significantly dominates at and after the third patent at the five-percent level in the Japanese data. The tipping point for the United

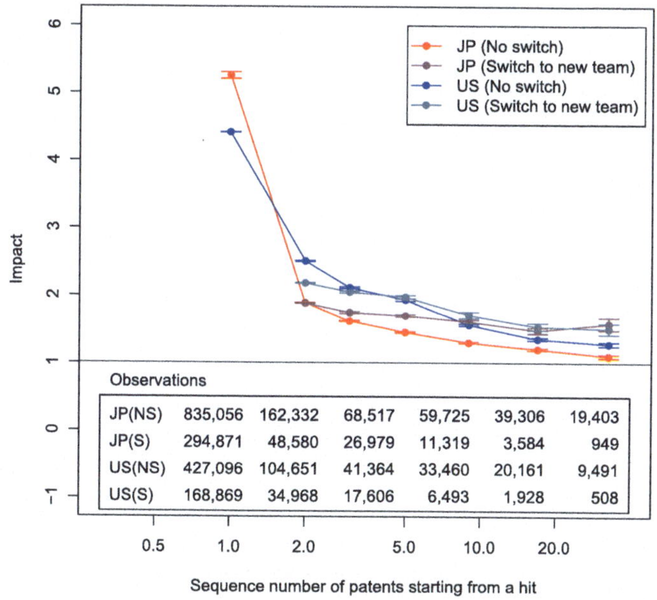

Fig. 3.6 The average impact of patents following hits. Hits are defined as patents in the top 10% of impact. The horizontal axis is the number of patents including a hit and all subsequent patents by the same team that created the hit. The hit is not necessarily the team's first patent. The vertical axis is the average impact. The horizontal axis is scaled such that the number of observations is greater than approximately 100. The red, greyish-red, blue, and greyish-blue lines correspond to Japanese "no switch", Japanese "switch to new team", US "no switch", and US "switch to new team". Standard errors are in brackets. The black horizontal line is impact = 1. (Source: [10])

States is the fifth patent. Note that because the sample sizes are not large enough after many repetitions, we cannot stably obtain significant results after the 11th patent for Japan and the 12th patent for the United States. As a result, individuals should switch teams after the second patent following a hit for Japanese patents and after the fourth patent for US patents. The data satisfy Prediction 3 based on this discussion.

To clearly demonstrate the effect of switching and discuss Prediction 3, let us define a measure, ρ_r.

$$\rho_r \equiv \frac{\text{Average impact of first patents created on new teams after (r-1)-th patents}}{\text{Average impact of r-th patents in teams}}.$$

If ρ_r is greater than one, the expected impact for the new team is larger than the r-th patent on the current team. Figure 3.7 plots ρ_r for each data set. Note that the plots are teams that had a hit, as in Fig. 3.6. The horizontal axis indicates the r-th patent after teams have hits. The definition of the repetition number is consistent with that in Fig. 3.6. The vertical axis represents ρ_r. The black horizontal line indicates $\rho_r = 1$. As subsequent patents continue to be filed, ρ_rs increases monotonically.

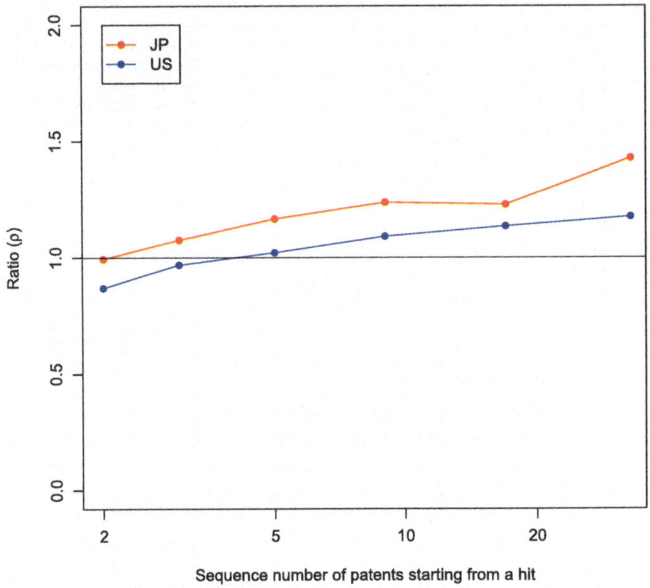

Fig. 3.7 The relationship between ρ_{r} and repetition. The horizontal axis is the number of patents including a hit and all subsequent patents by the same team that made the hit. The vertical axis represents the ratio (ρ_{r}). Hits are patents in the top 10% of impact. The horizontal axis is scaled such that the number of observations is greater than approximately 100. The black horizontal line indicates $\rho_{\mathrm{r}} = 1$. (Source: [10])

As noted above, ρ_{r} seems to exceed 1 at the third patent (the second patent after a hit) for Japanese patents. The threshold for US patents is five (the fourth patent after a hit).

It is natural that the line representing ρ_{r} depends on the threshold for a hit. The threshold is set at the top 10% for simplicity. The lines representing ρ_{r} show different thresholds in Fig. 3.8. There are four lines, each with a different threshold, for both Japan and the United States. These thresholds are "greater than 2", "greater than 4", "greater than 8", and "greater than 16" in terms of impact (note that "greater than 2" is roughly equivalent to the threshold for the top 10%). As indicated in Fig. 3.8, we do not observe a significant difference between thresholds in the Japanese data. However, it seems that the higher the threshold for a hit is, the lower ρ_{r} is in the US data. The Wilcoxon rank-sum tests are conducted between "greater than 2" and "greater than 16" for every repetition as a typical example. We find that ρ_{r} for "greater than 16" is significantly lower than that for "greater than 2". Thus, it is reasonable in the United States for people to postpone moving to a new team based on the level of patent impact.

Thus far, all predictions have been confirmed. This means that we have validated the innovator's dilemma, which has not been done before.

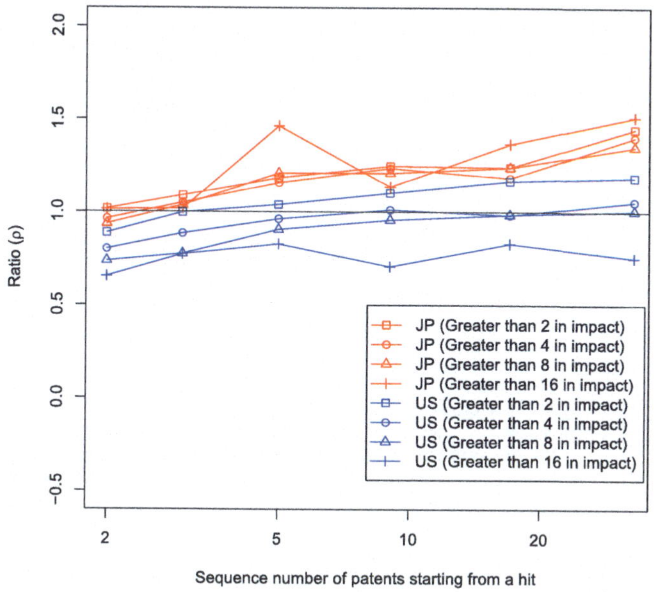

Fig. 3.8 The effect on ρ_{T} of the hit threshold. The horizontal axis represents the number of patents, including a hit and all subsequent patents by the same team that made the hit. The vertical axis depicts the ratio (ρ_{T}). There are four different thresholds for hits in this figure: greater than 2, 4, 8, and 16 in impact. The black horizontal line represents $\rho = 1$. (Source: [10])

We have not yet discussed other possible variables related to the experience of the team that could have been used instead of repetition. These include the age of inventors, the number of team patents, and the number of technology classes in which a team worked. These variables have already been investigated, and repetition and age are significantly related to the impact of patents [11]. Although repetition and age are also correlated, each variable separately affects impact. Therefore, repetition is a potent determinant of the impact of team patents.

3.4 Preventing Degeneration

The previous section explains that the creativity of teams declines on average, and therefore, inventors face a dilemma regarding whether to repeat a collaboration or switch teams. Since switching teams entails the cost of communication needed to build a new relationship and runs the risk of project failure, alleviating degeneration in repeat collaborations can help inventors. Here, we investigate two strategies for this purpose.

The first strategy is to develop technological diversity. Figure 3.9 plots the results with patents separated into two groups: the technologically inexperienced and experienced. If a patent at some repetition number has a technology that a

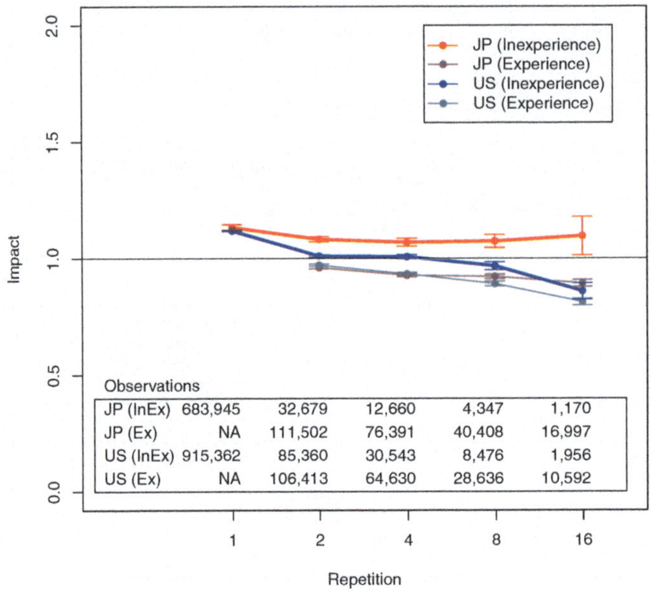

Observations					
JP (InEx)	683,945	32,679	12,660	4,347	1,170
JP (Ex)	NA	111,502	76,391	40,408	16,997
US (InEx)	915,362	85,360	30,543	8,476	1,956
US (Ex)	NA	106,413	64,630	28,636	10,592

Fig. 3.9 Average impact of repeat collaborations categorized by technological development. The horizontal axis depicts repeated team patents. The vertical axis represents the average impact. Standard errors are in brackets. "Technologically inexperienced" (InEx) means patents using technologies with which the team has no experience. "Technologically experienced" (Ex) means the opposite. The horizontal axis is scaled such that the number of observations is greater than approximately 100. The black horizontal line represents impact = 1. (Source: [10])

team has no experience with, it is categorized as "technologically inexperienced". Otherwise, it is categorized as "technologically experienced". The repetition number means the number of patents applied for by a given team. The plots include all teams regardless of whether patents are hits, although thus far we have considered only teams with hits. Since the results presented here are not limited to teams with hits, the prevention strategies can be broadly applied to all teams. The results reveal that repetitions in the inexperienced category are better than those in the experienced category. Moreover, there is no decline in the Japanese patent data.

Wilcoxon rank-sum tests are conducted between technologically inexperienced and experienced. We find that the inexperienced significantly dominates at the five-percent level at every repetition in both the Japanese and US data. Note that since there is insufficient sample size after many repetitions, the findings are not significant after the ninth patent for Japan and the 33rd patent for the United States. The standard errors in Fig. 3.9 appear large for the bin including the 16th repetition. This is because the bin is calculated for 9–16 repetitions. The standard errors for every repetition are smaller than those in Fig. 3.9. Thus, to avoid decline, a team should begin considering a new technological field in which they have no experience when possible.

The second strategy is developing inventor diversity. The definition of repeat collaborations thus far has been consecutive patents that have been published by a given team with the same participants. Repeat collaborations with shifts in inventors cannot be counted, that is, mixing teams under the original definition, because if the composition of inventors differs between two teams, these are considered to be different teams. Therefore, it is necessary to redefine repeat collaborations to consider this strategy. Repeat collaborations can be defined in another way based on pairs of inventors. Here, regardless of the other inventors involved in collaborations, repetitions are counted if two particular inventors are involved. For example, if there is a series of collaborations with inventors, such as inventors A, B, and C and inventors A, B, and D, there are two repeat collaborations for inventors A and B, but only one repeat collaboration for the other pairs of inventors. Using this definition, it is possible to consider the entry and exit of other inventors on teams involving two specific inventors. Figure 3.10 plots the results. There are two groups of results: inexperienced and experienced team setups. If a patent involves two inventors and they have not experienced a team setup (other teammate(s)) before, the patent is categorized as an inexperienced team setup and vice versa. The repetition number means the number of patents applied for by a given pair of

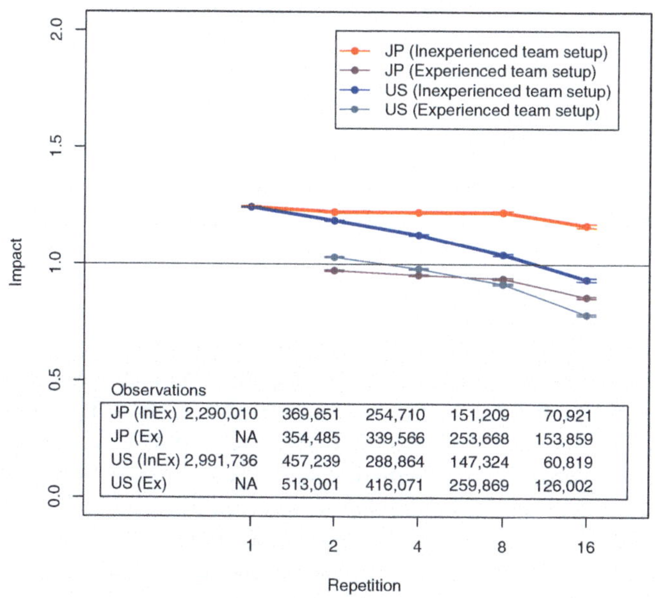

Fig. 3.10 The average impact of repeat collaborations categorized by the development of team members. The horizontal axis depicts repetitions by inventor pairs. The vertical axis represents the average impact. Standard errors are in brackets. "Inexperienced team setup" (InEx) means that some members other than target pair enter or exit. "Experienced team setup" (Ex) means the opposite. The horizontal axis is scaled such that the number of observations is greater than approximately 100. The black horizontal line represents impact = 1. (Source: [10])

inventors. The plots include all patents by pairs regardless of whether patents are hits. The results reveal that repeats with inexperienced team setups are better than those with experienced team setups. Moreover, the decline in general is substantially mitigated in the Japanese patent data.

We again conduct Wilcoxon rank-sum tests between inexperienced and experienced team setups. The inexperienced team setup significantly dominates at the five-percent level at every repetition in both the Japanese and US data. Note again that there is insufficient sample size after many repetitions. We do not obtain significant results after the 46th patent for Japan and the 30th patent for the United States. Therefore, changing a team setup when possible is always a good strategy to prevent degeneration. Guimerà et al.'s seminal work [8] demonstrates that repetitions negatively affect overall performance. Our study extends their work in the sense that changing a team setup has a positive effect at every repetition.

The two analyses, on technological diversity and inventor diversity, cannot be simply compared because their definitions of teams are different. Nevertheless, if we consider the gaps and the size of the error bars between the experienced and inexperienced teams, it appears plausible that mixing a team is more reliable than learning a new technology with an existing team because the relative size of the gaps in the standard errors of inventor diversity is larger than those of technological diversity.

3.5 Discussion

This chapter discussed repeat collaborations in creative projects and how they affect performance. Repeat collaborations have two contradictory aspects. The first is a positive aspect: team development or experience. The second is negative: team degeneration or decline. This dilemma has not previously been quantitatively analysed. This chapter has provided extensive quantitative analyses of the dilemma facing creative projects by using patent data from Japan and the United States.

Three predictions are proposed to validate the dilemma. Prediction 1 is that the more impactful the patent that a team completes, the longer the team will subsequently collaborate. Prediction 2 is that the impact of consecutive patents decreases after a team has a hit. Prediction 3 is that the expected impact of switching teams is greater than that of continuing to work on the same team at some point during subsequent patents. We validate these predictions with our data.

We then propose strategies to combat degeneration. The first is to develop technological diversity, and the second is to develop inventor diversity. When taken to the data, the two strategies are both shown to be effective.

The innovator's dilemma derives from the contradiction whereby inventors need to exploit previously obtained resources, including shared knowledge and team coordination, while simultaneously exploring new solutions that have not yet been created. From an exploitation perspective, it appears reasonable that teams will maximize the utility of their resources and achieve inventions that gradually degenerate. Therefore, it is straightforward to provide stimuli or perturbations to teams to expand their resources. However, shifting to an entirely new technological field and destroying team coordination eliminate the benefits of exploration. Our two analyses revealing the effect of considering new technologies and new team setups are evidence that there appear to be approaches to resolve the dilemma, especially when we carefully examine knowledge sharing and team coordination. In line with the discussion, a preceding experimental study indicated that dynamic teams are more adaptive than fixed teams, in the sense that the former explore the solution space without any intervention [5]. Additionally, another study revealed that dynamic teams are more promising than fixed teams if retention intervals are long [4]. Studying the innovator's dilemma with big data has only just begun, and there is considerable potential to further address it.

Furthermore, this analysis implies the applicability of the findings to other types of data. This chapter discusses repeated collaboration of inventor groups and the dilemma they face. Because the aim of any group, regardless of its purpose, is to achieve better performance, there is a trade-off between routines and dysfunction when a group does not adapt itself to situational changes. Previous studies have discussed routines in groups in other contexts, including political decision-making [12], research and development projects [14], or controlling unmanned aerial vehicles [4, 5]. Since routines and dysfunctions can be defined in these groups, it can be expected that the dilemma, i.e. when or how to mitigate dysfunction, can be studied on the basis of the framework proposed in this chapter.

This chapter discussed the relationship between the repeating collaborations and performance. However, retention between repetitions is not constant, and the degree of retention can affect performance. A prior study also discussed this from the perspective of dynamic team memberships, as in the present work, in a controlled environment [4]. A complementary study on retention using the data considered in this study represents an avenue for future work.

References

1. Christensen C. The innovator's dilemma: when new technologies cause great firms to fail. Boston: Harvard Business Press; 1997.
2. Delmestri G, Montanari F, Usai A. Reputation and strength of ties in predicting commercial success and artistic merit of independents in the Italian feature film industry*. J Manag Stud. 2005;42(5):975–1002.
3. Gersick CJG, Hackman JR. Habitual routines in task-performing groups. Organ Behav Hum Decis Process. 1990;47:65–97.
4. Gorman JC, Cooke NJ. Changes in team cognition after a retention interval: the benefits of mixing it up. J Exp Psychol Appl. 2011;17(4):303–19.
5. Gorman JC, Amazeen PG, Cooke NJ. Team coordination dynamics. Nonlinear Dynamics Psychol Life Sci. 2010;14(3):265–89.
6. Goto A, Motohashi K. Construction of a Japanese patent database and a first look at Japanese patenting activities. Res Policy. 2007;36(9):1431–42.

7. Griliches Z. R&D and productivity-the economic evidence. Chicago: The University of Chicago Press; 1998.
8. Guimera R, et al. Team assembly mechanisms determine collaboration network structure and team performance. Science. 2005;308(5722):697–702.
9. Hall BH, Jaffe AB, Trajtenberg M. The NBER patent citations data file: lessons, insights and methodological tools. National Bureau of Economic Research Working Paper 8498; 2001.
10. Inoue H. Evidence for a creative dilemma posed by repeated collaborations. PloS One. 2015;10(9):e0137418.
11. Inoue H, Liu Y. Revealing the intricate effect of collaboration on innovation. PLoS One. 2015;10(3):e0121973.
12. Janis IL. Groupthink. Boston: Houghton Mifflin School; 1982.
13. Jones BF. The burden of knowledge and the 'Death of the renaissance man': is innovation getting harder? NBER Working Paper Series; 2005.
14. Katz R. The effects of group longevity on project communication and performance. Admin Sci Q. 1982;27:81–104.
15. Kozlowski SWJ, Bell BS. Work groups and teams in organizations. In: Borman WC, Ilgen DR, Klimoski RJ, editors. Handbook of psychology, vol. 12. Hoboken: Wiley; 2003, p. 333–75.
16. Lai R, et al. Disambiguation and co-authorship networks of the U. S. patent inventor database (1975–2010). Technical report the Harvard Dataverse Network; 2012, p. 1–38.
17. Merton RK. The sociology of science: theoretical and empirical investigations. Chicago: University of Chicago Press; 1979.
18. Perretti F, Negro G. Mixing genres and matching people: a study in innovation and team composition in Hollywood. J Organ Behav. 2007;28(5):563–86.
19. Porac JF, et al. Human capital heterogeneity, collaborative relationships, and publication patterns in a multidisciplinary scientific alliance: a comparative case study of two scientific teams. Res Policy. 2004;33(4):661–78.
20. Reagans R, Zuckerman E, McEvily B. How to make the team: social networks vs. demography as criteria for designing effective teams. Admin Sci Q. 2004;49(1):101–33.
21. Schwab A, Miner AS. Learning in hybrid-project systems: the effects of project performance on repeated collaboration. Acad Manag J. 2008;51:1117–49.
22. Skilton PF, Dooley KJ. The effects of repeat collaboration on creative abrasion. Acad Manag Rev. 2010;35(1):118–34.
23. Uzzi B, Spiro J. Collaboration and creativity: the small world problem1. Am J Sociol. 2005;111(2):447–504.
24. Wuchty S, Jones BF, Uzzi B. The increasing dominance of teams in production of knowledge. Science. 2007;316(5827):1036–9.

Chapter 4
Agglomeration of Establishment Location

4.1 Introduction

This chapter discusses the geographical aggregation of business establishments that have published patents. The findings in this chapter mainly rely on the author's previous work [5]. Most figures and tables are replicated with proper permission from the publisher. The main text is modified to fit the context of this book.

Chapters 2 and 3 address collaborations as recorded in patents. These are explicit collaborations because they are recorded. However, in addition to explicit collaborations, implicit collaborations, i.e. collaborations without records, can also exist. Such implicit collaborations cannot be observed directly. However, if collaborations occur under certain conditions, we can expect actors to place themselves in these conditions because they wish to use collaboration to obtain more innovation.

This chapter focuses on geographical proximity as one such condition. Silicon Valley is repeatedly used as an example: geographical proximity can promote knowledge spillovers and is a determinant of agglomerations [3, 6, 8]. This can be applicable not only to knowledge-based creative actors but also to firms in general. Indeed, manufacturing industries in the United Kingdom and Japan are localized [2, 7].

Empirical works have addressed geographical agglomeration. The intensity of R&D investment is positively related to the extent of industrial agglomeration [8]. Moreover, the intensity of citation relationships between industries positively relates to the extent of co-agglomeration between the pair of industries [3]. These studies use industry-level data and examine which industries are located closely to one another. However, even at the actor, i.e. business establishment, level, there are knowledge spillovers, and such agglomeration can occur within a given industry.

Another study examines the localization of R&D laboratories that have high demand for external knowledge [1]. The authors use address information of R&D laboratories from the *Directory of American Research and Technology* and find that

H. Inoue, *Co-patenting: An Analytic Tool for Cooperative Research and Development*, Evolutionary Economics and Social Complexity Science 21,
https://doi.org/10.1007/978-4-431-54807-2_4

R&D laboratories are significantly localized in most industries. They also identify core clusters of R&D laboratories in the U.S. and localized spillovers within the identified clusters.

However, since their data focus on local patterns, the overall localization pattern, such as at the nationwide, is not discussed.

The actors considered in Chaps. 2 and 3 are inventors or firms. However, business establishments can be extracted from Japanese patent data. Japanese patent applications enable us to construct an establishment-level database: inventors register the address of the establishments to which they belong as the "inventor's address". The details of the data construction are reported in Sect. 4.2.

Based on the above background, this chapter discusses the localization of business establishments. We use Japanese data to examine the overall pattern of agglomeration. In addition, we also examine interindustry differences. The literature on industrial agglomeration focuses on manufacturing. However, service industries also have inventions and patents. Therefore, comparisons between manufacturing and service industries are also interesting.

Furthermore, such industrial comparisons have different implications. We expect that advanced industries or technologies require more intensive knowledge spillovers than other industries. Therefore, the agglomeration of establishments could be stronger. Further aspects to consider are frequency and quality. Establishments that create more or higher-quality patents require more knowledge spillovers.

The analysis in this chapter uses distance-based analysis, developed by Duranton and Overman [2], to investigate the agglomeration of establishments. This analysis utilizes the distribution of bilateral distance between all pairs of actors. The critical idea is to compare the distribution of bilateral distances with the counterfactual distribution generated by a random sampling of all establishment locations. Regarding the potential sites of establishments, all establishments from the microdata in the Establishment and Enterprise Census are used.

4.2 Data

This work uses the Institute of Intellectual Property (IIP) patent database [4], which includes Japanese patent publications (the Patent Gazette). As mentioned in Chaps. 2 and 3, this database includes basic patent information, such as patent IDs, publication dates, names and addresses of applicants, and names and addresses of inventors. The database also includes citation information on each patent, such as the number of times the patent has been cited. An establishment-level database is used by considering all patents published from 1993 to 2008.

This chapter focuses on the localization of patent-creating establishments. Since patents do not explicitly include information about establishments, we need to

Table 4.1 Data summary. (Source: [5])

No. of patents	1,967,361
Number of patents applied for by establishments	1,189,262
Number of applicants (firms)	56,592
Number of establishments with patents	74,452
Overall number of establishments (census)	5,722,559

identify the patent-creating establishments from the patent database, which can be done by exploiting an aspect of the Japanese patent application: inventors register the address of the establishments to which they belong as the "inventor's address".

The algorithm is as follows. First, firms are identified by the name and address of the applicants. Firms can be identified if an applicant name includes the term "company limited" or "kabushiki gaisha" in Japanese. This operation simultaneously excludes relatively small firms, such as private limited companies, because the spelling of their corporate status is different. Then, establishments are identified. If the firm's name is included in the inventor's address, the address can be regarded as the address of the establishment owned by the firm found in the application name.

Using this identification method, we build our database. Table 4.1 provides a summary of the data set. It includes 1,967,361 patents. Identified establishments applied for 1,189,262 patents. There are 56,592 firm applicants and 74,452 establishments.

On the other hand, the Establishment and Enterprise Census in 2006 states that there are 5,722,559 establishments in Japan. The Establishment and Enterprise Census includes the address, number of employees, and industry code information of each establishment. Then, the establishments' addresses are converted into locations with latitude and longitude information. All establishment data are necessary because the analysis requires the potential sites of establishments with patents. Namely, in the analyses, we assume that all establishments are considered potential establishments with patents. The details of the analysis are explained in Sect. 4.3.

Figure 4.1 depicts a map of establishments with patents identified by our methodology. As the map shows, the identified establishments are widely distributed across Japan.

4.3 Empirical Strategy

To examine the localization of establishments with patents, we use Duranton and Overman's distance-based approach [2]. First, the distribution of bilateral distances is calculated between all pairs of establishments with patents; then, the counterfactual distribution is generated by the random assignment of locations from potential sites, i.e. all establishments.

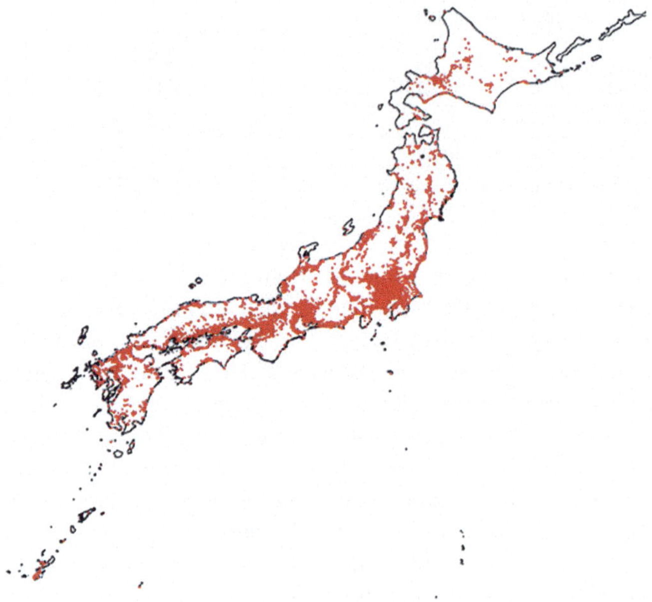

Fig. 4.1 Map of establishments with patents. (Source: [5])

K-Density Approach

The details of the algorithm are as follows. Let n be the number of establishments that have applied for at least one patent. Then, we have $n(n-1)/2$ pairs of the establishments. Let d_{ij} be the great circle distance between the pair of establishments i and j. The density of bilateral distances at any point d is assumed to be

$$K(d) = \frac{1}{n(n-1)h} \Sigma_{i=1}^{n-1} \Sigma_{j=i+1}^{n} f\left(\frac{d-d_{ij}}{h}\right), \tag{4.1}$$

where h is the optimal bandwidth, which is set to the same value as in Silverman [9], and f is the Gaussian kernel function.

Counterfactual Distribution and Statistical Testing

Establishments have a tendency to agglomerate because economic activities have geographical frictions. Therefore, to precisely detect the localization of patent-creating establishments, it is necessary to control for the localization of overall economic activity. To this end, a counterfactual distribution is created based on locations of establishments by randomly choosing locations from all potential sites as a reference. Then, the counterfactual distribution is compared with the actual distribution.

A two-sided confidence interval is created to test the localization of patent-creating establishments. n sites are randomly chosen from the potential sites and used to estimate the K-density in the counterfactual situation. Importantly, this random selection is iterated 1,000 times, and we thereby obtain the "global confidence bands" introduced by [2]. Here, an upper confidence band $K^U(d)$ is defined such that 95% of observations lie below the upper confidence band. Then, $K^L(d)$ is defined such that 95% of observations lie above the lower confidence band. The sample selections for the boundary are performed in the entire distance range, which is 0–180 km.

We say that actual patent-creating establishments are globally localized at the 5% level when actual patent-creating establishments have $\widehat{K}(d) > K^U(d)$, where $d \in [0, 180]$. Here, note that d is an integer. In addition, as with [2], the extent of localization is defined as follows:

$$\Gamma = \Sigma_{d \in [0,180]} \max\{\widehat{K}(d) - K^U(d), 0\}. \tag{4.2}$$

Baseline Results

Figure 4.2 provides heat maps. The left panel represents overall economic activity. The colour of each cell shows its share relative to all establishments in Japan.

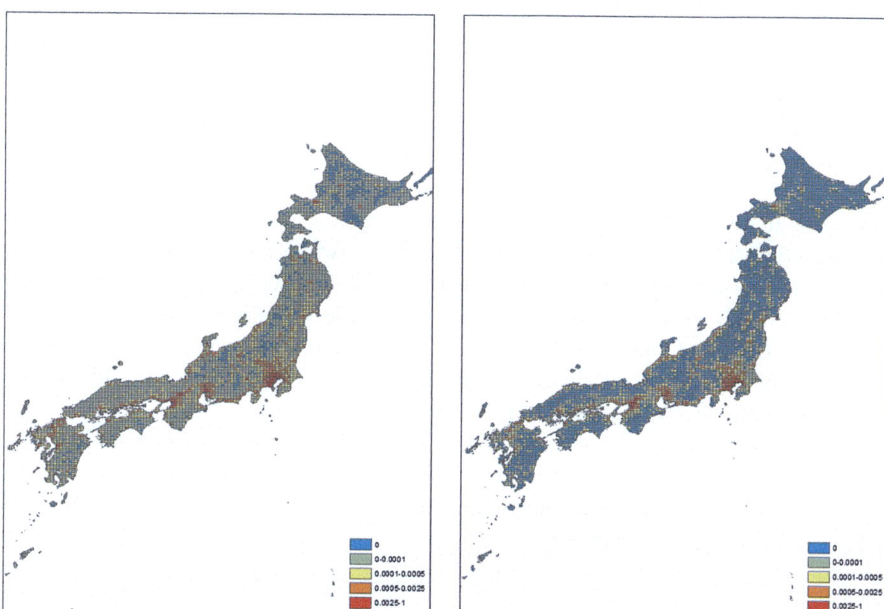

Fig. 4.2 Map of all economic activity and patent-creating activities. Left panel: All economic activity. Right panel: Patent-creating activities. (Source: [5])

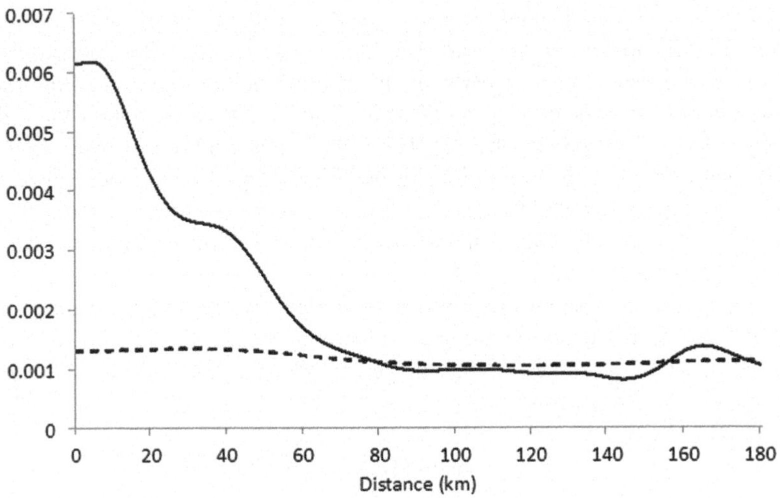

Fig. 4.3 Results of the baseline analysis. The vertical axis is density. (Source: [5])

Blue indicates a relatively smaller share of establishments, while red indicates a relatively larger share of establishments. The panel shows that economic activities are distributed throughout Japan, although we observe some concentration in metropolitan areas. The right panel shows patent-creating activities. The colours of cells in this panel have the same meaning as in the left panel. By comparing the right and left panels, we find that patent-creating activities are more concentrated in metropolitan areas.

Figure 4.3 shows the baseline result, which corresponds to the above-mentioned concentration. The solid line in the figure presents the K-density of the actual distribution, and the dashed lines represent the global confidence bands. The K-density is above the upper global confidence band for every distance within a range less than approximately 80 km. Therefore, patent-creating establishments are significantly localized. This result indicates that knowledge spillovers act as a force of agglomeration between establishments that create knowledge.

Although the result indicates that patent-creating establishments are localized within the 0–80 km range, 80 km could be considered large for a local cluster. However, the transportation system in Japan is well-developed, which could expand the distance at which collaboration is possible.

The results also show that there is a strong peak at 20 km and that the density then declines rapidly. This implies that patent-creating establishments are highly localized within a short distance of one another and that knowledge spillovers require a short distance to occur.

4.4 Heterogeneity Between Patent-Creating Establishments

In the baseline analysis, patent-creating establishments are considered homogeneous. However, there are meaningful differences between patent-creating establishments, for example, in how the localization differs between industries or patent classes and how establishment productivity affects localization, among others. These findings are interesting because some of the differences might arise from the demand for knowledge spillovers. The differences between establishments are discussed in this section.

Controlling for Industrial Localization

The baseline analysis uses establishments in all industries as potential sites for patent-creating establishments. However, if there are many patent-creating establishments in a specific industry that have a strong tendency to localize, our results might only capture such localization and not the overall localization of patent-creating establishments. To address this issue, it is important to assess the effects of localization for each industry since the distributions may differ across industries. A within-industry analysis can be performed to control for such industrial heterogeneity. In essence, only observations in a given industry are used for each analysis. To this end, we need to identify the industry to which each patent-creating establishment belongs. This can be achieved by using industry information from a large-scale, firm-level database provided by Tokyo Shoko Research (TSR). The TSR data cover 826,169 Japanese firms, which is over half the total firms in Japan. We can identify the applicant firms' industries using the TSR data with the patent database using the firm's name and address information. Note that there are significant numbers of patent-creating establishments that belong to the non-manufacturing sector. In the data, approximately 33% of patent-creating establishments are in non-manufacturing industries. The industries are identified by two-digit codes to obtain sufficient sample sizes. In addition, industries with fewer than 10 establishments with patents are omitted.

The K-density is modified to analyse the within-industry localization. Let S^I be a set of establishments that have applied for at least one patent and belong to industry $I \in \mathrm{I}$, where I represents a set of industries. Let n_I be the number of patent-creating establishments in industry I. Similarly, let d_{ij} be the great circle distance between establishments i and j in set S^I. Here, the density of bilateral distances at any point d for industry I is newly defined as

$$\widehat{K^I}(d) = \frac{1}{n_I(n_I-1)h}\Sigma_{i=1}^{n_I-1}\Sigma_{j=i+1}^{n_I} f(\frac{d-d_{ij}}{h}). \qquad (4.3)$$

Since the counterfactual distribution should also be in the same industry, the site of every establishment in industry $I \in \mathrm{I}$ is considered a potential site for patent-creating establishments.

There are 83.6% industries (61 of the total of 73 industries) with localization significant at the 5% level. Since patent-creating establishments are more localized within these same industries, the baseline result is not caused by specific industries exhibiting strong agglomeration tendencies. Regarding the difference between manufacturing and non-manufacturing industries, 91% of manufacturing industries are localized, while 79% of non-manufacturing industries are localized.

Although the non-manufacturing industries exhibit a lower number of localizations, this does not necessarily mean that knowledge spillovers play a lesser role in these cases. As [7] shows, service industries tend to be more localized than other industries, and the counterfactual distributions are highly localized in service industries. Therefore, the strong localization of the counterfactual is likely the explanation for the lower number of localizations.

Differences by Patent Technology Classes

Localization may differ between establishments with different patent technology classes. This is meaningful because the demand for knowledge spillovers may vary with the patent technology class, and one could expect that inventions in higher technology classes require strong knowledge spillovers. Therefore, establishments in high-technology classes are most likely strongly localized.

The K-density estimation is modified for the technology-level analysis. Let S^A be a set of establishments that have applied for at least one patent in patent technology class $A \in \mathrm{A}$, where A represents a set of patent technology classes. Let n_A be the number of patent-creating establishments in patent technology class A. Similarly, let d_{ij} be the great circle distance between establishments i and j in set S^A. The estimator at any point d for patent technology class A is

$$\widehat{K^A}(d) = \frac{1}{n_A(n_A-1)h} \Sigma_{i=1}^{n_A-1} \Sigma_{j=i+1}^{n_A} f(\frac{d-d_{ij}}{h}). \tag{4.4}$$

All establishments are potential sites for patent-creating establishments for the counterfactual distribution.

The patent technology classes are identified by the first three letters of the International Patent Classification (IPC). This classification includes 120 patent technology classes.

Figure 4.4 shows the number of patent technology classes that are localized at each distance. All 120 patent classes are localized in the range of 0–60 km. After 60 km, the number of localized patent classes declines gradually. This pattern is similar to industrial localization in the manufacturing industry [2, 7].

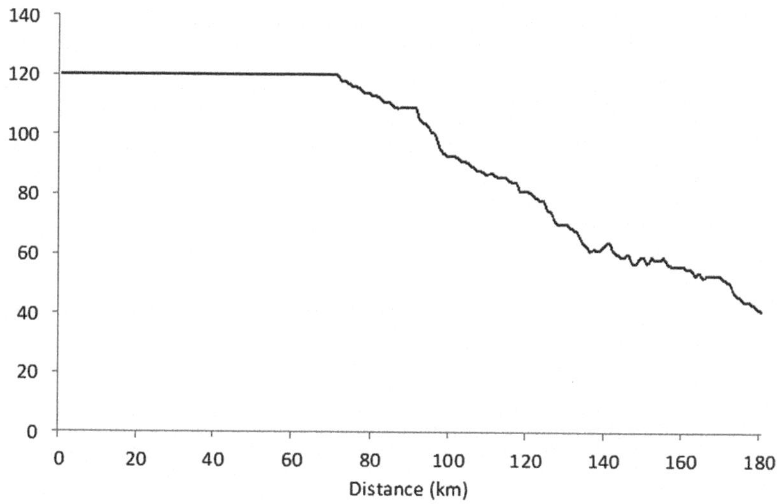

Fig. 4.4 Number of localized patent classes by distance. The vertical axis is the number of localized patent classes. (Source: [5])

Table 4.2 Top 10 patent technology classes in localization. (Source: [5])

Rank	IPC	technology class	Gamma
1	B64	Aircraft;aviation;astronautics	0.348
2	G07	Checking devices	0.346
3	G04	Horology	0.329
4	G06	Computing;calculating;counting	0.315
5	H03	Basic electronic circuitry	0.313
6	G11	Information storage	0.312
7	H04	Electric communication technique	0.306
8	G12	Instrument details	0.295
9	B42	Bookbinding;albums;files;special printed matter	0.290
10	B43	Writing or drawing implements;bureau accessories	0.287

The extent of the localization is defined as Γ, and we can use it to examine the intensity of localization. Table 4.2 shows the top 10 patent technology classes. Most of the patent technology classes are high-tech industries, such as aircraft, aviation, and astronautics.

Table 4.3 shows the bottom 10 patent technology classes. In this table, the patent technology classes are low-tech industries, such as butchering, meat treatment, and poultry and fish processing. These tables clearly show the difference in the requirements for knowledge spillovers.

Table 4.3 Bottom 10 patent technology classes in localization. (Source: [5])

Rank	IPC	technology class	Gamma
1	A22	Butchering;meat treatment;processing poultry or fish	0.000
2	C06	Explosives;matches	0.031
3	B27	Working or preserving wood or similar material; nailing or stapling machines in general	0.058
4	A24	Tobacco;cigars;cigarettes;smokers' requisites	0.083
5	C21	Metallurgy of iron	0.086
6	F26	Drying	0.094
7	F22	Steam generation	0.094
8	C05	Fertilizers;manufacture thereof	0.096
9	B22	Casting;powder metallurgy	0.096
10	B02	Crushing, pulverizing, or disintegrating;preparatory of grain for milling	0.105

We have yet to validate the hypothesis that the degree of technological advancement may correlate with localization. Therefore, it is desirable to use an objective value to indicate technological advancement. The level of R&D investment is an appropriate value. Arguably, a higher-technology class requires more investment in invention. Therefore, the level of technology is defined as the ratio of R&D investment over total sales.

The Basic Survey of Japanese Business Structure and Activities enables us to calculate the ratio of R&D investment over total sales in each patent technology class. The Basic Survey of Japanese Business Structure and Activities covers firms with more than 50 employees and capital stock of over 30 million yen and includes each firm's sales, R&D investment, and industry code. Then, R&D intensity can be calculated by dividing the aggregated R&D investment by the aggregated sales for each three-digit-level industrial code. Since the firm survey contains industrial codes and the patents have technology classes, we need a concordance list. We thus resort to an additional database in conjunction with the TSR firm database. This new database includes the industry code (JSIC) for each firm. We can obtain the industry information for each patent by combining the TSR data with the patent database by using the firm's name and address information. Finally, by using information on industry-level R&D investment shares and calculating the weighted average of the R&D investment shares based on the above-mentioned industry composite, we can calculate the technology levels.

Figure 4.5 shows the relationship between the degree of localization and R&D investment. The horizontal line shows the R&D investment share, and the vertical line refers to the degree of localization in each technology class. The solid line represents the linear fitted line. We observe a clear positive relationship. Furthermore, the correlation coefficient is 0.41, and the statistical test shows that it is significant at the 1% level. This result indicates that establishments in high-technology classes are more localized to acquire knowledge spillovers.

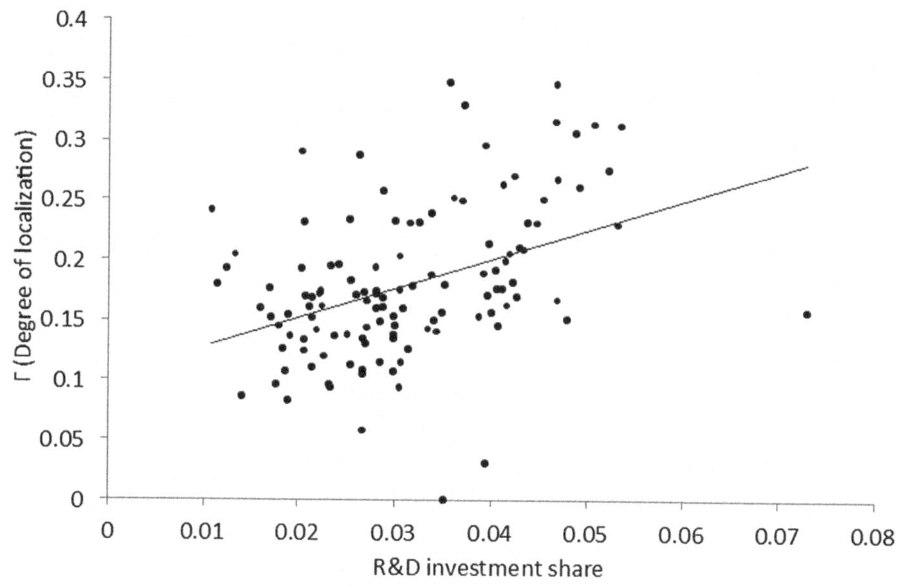

Fig. 4.5 Relationship between R&D investment share and degree of localization. (Source: [5])

Differences by Establishment-Level Productivity

Establishments are heterogeneous in productivity, and we expect that the more productive establishments are, the more external knowledge they require. In this section, we consider two measures of productivity: the number of patent publications and the number of citations received. The number of patent publications measures establishments' patent productivity in terms of quantity, and the number of patent citations received measures establishments' patent productivity in terms of quality. In economics in general, productivity normally indicates sales or value added per worker or unit of capital. However, the numbers of patents and citations are simply used here.

The density function is modified again as follows:

$$\widehat{K}(d) = \frac{1}{h\Sigma_{i=1}^{n-1}\Sigma_{i+1}^{n} w(i)w(j)} \Sigma_{i=1}^{n-1}\Sigma_{j=i+1}^{n} w(i)w(j) f\left(\frac{d-d_{ij}}{h}\right), \tag{4.5}$$

where $w(i)$ is the weight on productivity for establishment i. The weight is either the number of patents or the number of total citations received.

The upper panel of Fig. 4.6 depicts the results for quantitative productivity weighted by the number of patents. The solid line in the figure represents the K-density weighted by the number of patents, and the dashed lines represent the global confidence bands. For every distance in the 0–85 km range, the K-density is above

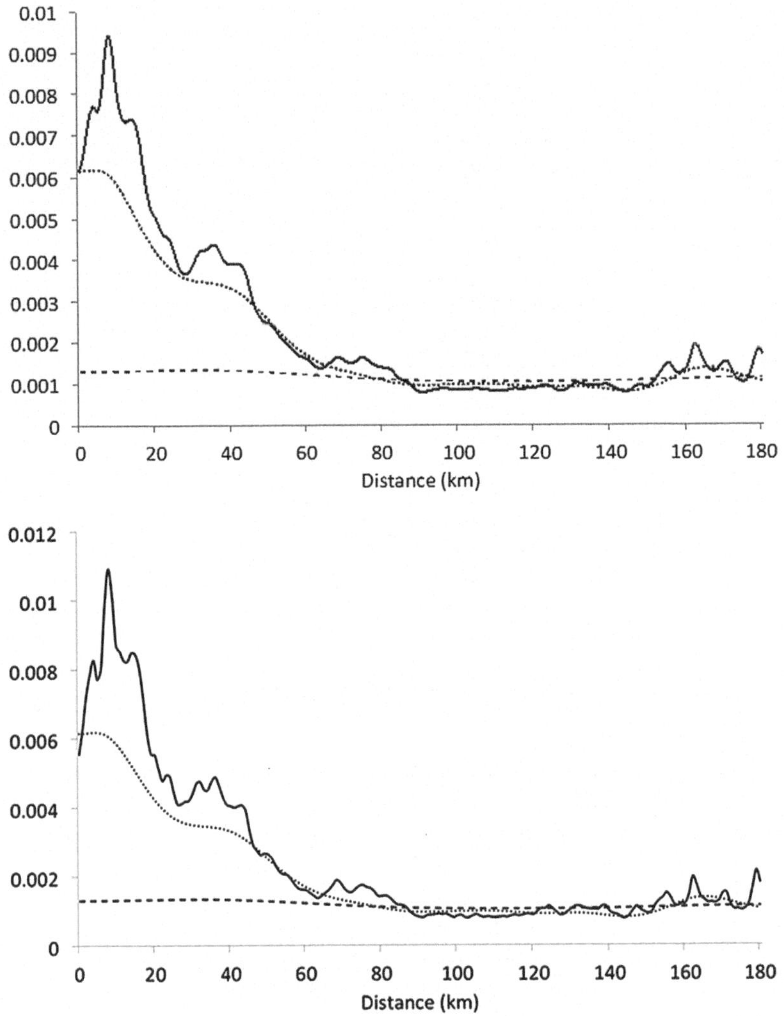

Fig. 4.6 Results weighted by establishment productivity. Top panel: Weighted by number of patents. Bottom panel: Weighted by number of patent citations. Vertical axes in both panels are density. (Source: [5])

the upper global confidence band. Thus, the distribution is localized in the 0–85 km range, even if we weight by the number of patents created.

The baseline K-density is also depicted as the dotted line in Fig. 4.6. We clearly observe that the weighted density is above the unweighted K-density within a 0–50 km range. The extent of localization between weighted and unweighted results yields $\Gamma = 0.221$ and $\Gamma = 0.163$, respectively. Therefore, the weighted distribution is larger than the baseline result. This indicates that the more establishments publish patents, the more localized they are, implying that productive establishments require knowledge transfers.

Next, we turn to productivity measured in terms of quality. These results are presented in the bottom panel of Fig. 4.6. The solid line in the figure represents the K-density weighted by the total number of citations received. The dashed lines represent the global confidence bands, and the dotted line represents the baseline K-density. The results present a similar shape to the previous result obtained for quantity. In the close range of 0–80 km, the establishments are localized, and the weighted density is more localized than the unweighted density. The Γs are $\Gamma = 0.245$ for the weighted and $\Gamma = 0.163$ for the baseline, and the former is clearly greater than the latter. We thus reconfirm that productive establishments are more localized than others.

4.5 Discussion

This chapter investigates the localization of patent-creating establishments in Japan. Using the K-density approach [2], the following results are found. (1) Establishments are significantly localized in the range of 0–80 km. (2) Establishments are significantly localized in each industry. (3) Localization is found for all patent technology classes, but the extent of localization has a positive relationship with the level of technology. (4) Localization is stronger in more productive establishments, measured in terms of quantity or quality. All of these results indicate that geographical proximity is important for patent-creating establishments if they are knowledge intensive.

The results suggest that establishments tend to localize to enjoy the benefit of knowledge spillovers and collaborations. Therefore, agglomeration is a condition for creative collaboration.

References

1. Carlino GA, et al. The agglomeration of R&D labs. Working Paper Series 12–22. Federal Reserve Bank of Philadelphia; 2012.
2. Duranton G, Overman HG. Testing for localization using micro-geographic data. Rev Econ Stud. 2005;72(4):1077–106.
3. Ellison G, Glaeser EL, Kerr WR. What causes industry agglomeration? Am Econ Rev. 2010;105:889–927.
4. Goto A, Motohashi K. Construction of a Japanese patent database and a first look at Japanese patenting activities. Res Policy. 2007;36(9):1431–42.
5. Inoue H, Nakajima K, Saito Y. Localization of knowledge-creating establishments. Jpn World Econ. 2017;43:23–9.
6. Marshall A. Principles of economics. London: Macmillan; 1920.
7. Nakajima K, Saito YU, Uesugi I. Measuring economic localization: evidence from Japanese firm-level data. J Jpn Int Econ. 2012;26(2):201–20.
8. Rosenthal SS, Strange WC. The determinants of agglomeration. J Urban Econ. 2001;50(2):191–229.
9. Silverman BW. Density estimation for statistics and data analysis. New York: Chapman and Hall; 1986.

Chapter 5
Agglomeration of Establishment Co-patenting

5.1 Introduction

Chapters 2 and 3 discuss networks with explicit collaborations recorded in patents. In addition, location agglomeration is discussed in Chap. 4. The current chapter returns to explicit collaborations and analyses how business establishments with co-patenting are aggregated geographically. The findings in this chapter mainly rely on the author's prior work [10]. Most figures and tables are replicated with proper permission from the publisher. The main text is modified to fit the context of this book.

Since individuals engaged in collaborative efforts intensively exchange ideas and information, such efforts directly indicate knowledge spillovers. Since it is important to identify the conditions under which collaborations occur, this chapter analyses the localization of collaborations as one such condition. If collaborations are localized, this will clearly demonstrate the presence of geographical frictions in knowledge spillovers.

The analysis also allows us investigate the death of distance. Information now flows electronically and instantaneously, which reduces distance frictions in information transfer. Distance frictions in knowledge transfer may thus disappear, and new ideas immediately spread throughout the world [3]. Recent empirical evidence obtained from patent citation data indicates that geographical frictions associated with international borders have declined [7].

Patent citations can be interpreted as the transfer of codified knowledge and are easily accessed online. Several studies have examined the localization of knowledge spillovers using patent citations [11, 13, 15, 20]. In contrast, collaborations essentially involve transfers of tacit knowledge and require face-to-face communications that demand researchers' actual presence. Thus, one can expect that geographical distance continues to play a substantial and significant role in knowledge spillovers

H. Inoue, *Co-patenting: An Analytic Tool for Cooperative Research and Development*, Evolutionary Economics and Social Complexity Science 21,
https://doi.org/10.1007/978-4-431-54807-2_5

achieved through collaborations. This chapter examines the death of distance using long-term data from 1986 to 2005.

This chapter also discusses firm-border effects in collaborations. As several studies have noted (e.g. [8, 17]), collaborations between firms are considered difficult because firms' interests conflict and unwanted transfers of knowledge and organizational secrets significantly harm the competitiveness of firms. Comparing inter- and intra-firm collaborations allows us to quantitatively evaluate firm-border effects in collaborations. As introduced in Chap. 4, establishment-level collaboration data can be applied to the topics considered in this chapter. These establishment-level data also allow us to investigate firm-border effects on the geographical friction in collaborations for the first time in the literature.

To assess the geographic proximity of establishment-level collaborations, we should consider the geographic proximity of research establishments overall. Such an analysis was used in Chap. 4, and the K-density approach [5] is revisited here. Since knowledge-creating establishments are concentrated in certain areas [2, 4], a naive measurement of the geographic proximity between collaborating establishments inevitably reflects the proximity of establishments. To control for the geographic proximity of establishments, we need to consider counterfactual collaborations in which establishments choose partners regardless of distance. These counterfactual collaborations reflect the geographic proximity of the establishments. Then, the actual collaborations are compared with the counterfactual collaborations.

5.2 Data

In this chapter, we use the same data as in Chap. 4. However, this chapter focuses not only on the locations of establishments but also their collaborations. Therefore, an establishment-level collaboration data set is constructed based on the Institute of Intellectual Property (IIP) patent database (DB) [6]. The patent records contained in this database range from 1986 to 2005. We use the application date instead of the publication date. The publication date differs from the application date because of the time required to review applications. The application date is preferable for appropriately capturing the time when R&D activities actually occurred because it is closer to the time when the research was actually conducted.

After the establishments are identified, collaboration between establishments is identified as follows. If a patent includes different establishments, the establishments are assumed to have collaborated. This chapter decomposes every collaboration into bilateral collaborative relationships. That is, if a patent includes more than two establishments, all bilateral combinations between establishments are registered. For example, if a patent includes three establishments, A, B, and C, there are three bilateral collaborations between A and B, B and C, and C and A.

One might wonder what the effect of inventors moving to another office is, which could bias the sample. Namely, an inventor transfers from an establishment during a collaboration but before the patent has been applied for. She ultimately

Table 5.1 Data summary. (Source: [9])

No. of patents	1,967,361
Number of patents applied for by establishments	1,189,262
Number of patents applied for by collaborating establishments	93,939
Number of patents (intra-firm collaborations)	37,865
Number of patents (inter-firm collaborations)	56,074
Number of establishments	74,452
Number of firms	56,592
Number of single-establishment firms	46,904
Number of multi-establishment firms	9,688

reports her new establishment in the patent application, and the location is thus not accurate. This could bias the sample, but we conclude that the effect is small. Based on the literature, we can calculate the probability of uncertain collaboration reports by using the frequency of the inventor's transfer and the average duration of the invention process. The data indicate that 22.4% of researchers transfer establishments within 16 years [18]. In addition, in Japan, on average, 18 months pass between when a project is started until a patent application is filed [19]. Thus, we can roughly estimate that 2.3% $(= 1 - (1 - 0.224)18/12/16)$ of workers transferred establishments within in an 18-month period. The magnitude is thus small.

Table 5.1 provides a summary of the data set. Out of 1,967,361 patents, we have establishment data for 1,189,262. Firms apply for 60.4% of all patents. In OECD countries, firms apply for approximately 80% of patents [16]. This share is thus lower in our data, but we have sufficient observations for analysis. The identification procedure identifies 56,592 firms and 74,452 establishments.

Establishments applied for 1,189,262 patents. Of these, 7.9% (93,939 patents) involve establishment-level collaborations. Of the collaborative patents, 59.7% (56,074 patents) involve collaborations between different firms (i.e. inter-firm collaborations).

Furthermore, we can identify how many establishments are recorded for each firm. The data set includes 9,688 multi-establishment firms and 46,904 single-establishment firms. Obviously, if a firm does not publish patents during the period of analysis, we cannot obtain these data.

5.3 Empirical Strategy

The empirical strategy is in line with that in Chap. 4. Establishments with patents are concentrated in certain areas [2, 4, 9]. Therefore, even if establishments chose partners irrespective of distance (e.g. at random), establishments that collaborate would usually be located a short distance apart. To appropriately assess the proximity of collaborating establishments, we must control for the overall geographic proximity of research establishments and consider counterfactual collaborations. In Chap. 4, counterfactual samples are chosen from among all establishments (including non-patent-creating establishments) in Japan. By contrast, counterfactual collaborations are chosen from among patent-creating establishments that reflect the approximate locations of the establishments in question.

A more rigorous expression of the test is as follows. Let S^A be a set of establishments that have applied for at least one patent in patent technology class $A \in \mathrm{A}$ over the entire period of analysis, where A represents a set of patent technology classes. Let P_A be the set of patent applications that is submitted by the collaborating establishments, let $p_{ij} \wedge A \in P_A$ be a patent application that is submitted by collaborating establishments i and j in technology class A, and let n_A^p be the number of patent applications submitted by the collaborating establishments in technology class A.

Here, S^A is defined as the set of potential collaboration partners in patent technology class A. As counterfactual collaborations, we randomly choose n_A^p pairs of establishments from S^A.

There is a more conservative way to construct our samples. We could restrict our attention to establishments that have at least one experience of collaboration. However, the results remained qualitatively unchanged under this alternative definition.

In the analysis, the first three letters of the International Patent Classification (IPC) are used to categorize the patents. Since a patent often has multiple IPCs, the primary IPC is assigned to each patent. There are 120 patent technology classes in the data.

The counterfactual collaborations represent a situation in which establishments choose their partners at random. Thus, the counterfactual collaborations capture the geographic proximity of the establishments in each technology class.

However, there is an inevitable limitation of the approach. If establishments choose their locations because they expect future collaborations form locating there, establishments will choose locations that have many potential collaborators. Therefore, the counterfactual collaborations will be more localized than establishments without such expectations. This could lead to underestimates of the localization of collaborations.

The K-density approach [5] is revisited. This method was originally developed to test the localization of the manufacturing establishments' locations. Here, it is applied to collaborations. As a first step, all of the bilateral distances between the collaborating establishments are calculated. This is the actual distribution. Then, as the second step, counterfactual collaborations are created such that each establishment randomly chooses its partner. Based on the counterfactual distance distributions, we construct a confidence interval band and then test the actual distribution. The details of kernel density are omitted here but are provided in Sect. 4.3.

5.4 Baseline Results

Figure 5.1 shows the baseline result. For every distance in the 0–100 km range, the K-density is above the upper global confidence band. Thus, the collaborations are localized within the 0–100 km range, and this result is significant at the 5% level.

The localization tendency may vary across technology classes. Thus, strong localization tendencies in a small number of technology classes may cause this overall localization. To address this issue, we can test for differences in the localization tendencies between patent technology classes. Namely, the same analysis is conducted for each technology class.

The localization for each distance d is assessed. If $\widehat{K_A}(d) > \underline{K}_A^U(d)$ at distance d, patent technology class A is localized at distance d. Here, $\widehat{K_A}(d)$ is the actual density of class A, and $K_A^U(d)$ is the upper bound of counterfactual collaborations. Figure 5.2 shows the number of technology classes that are localized at each distance. At shorter distances, collaborations are localized in 108 of the 120 technology classes. At distances of more than 100 km, the number of localized technology classes begins to decline.

Table 5.2 shows the frequency distributions of Γ that represent the extent of localization in each technology class. Most technology classes exhibit localization, but the value of Γ ranges from 0 to 0.5.

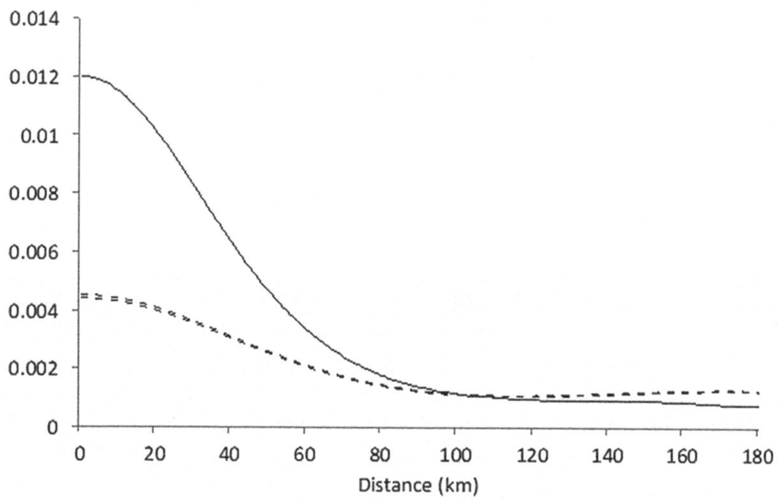

Fig. 5.1 K-density of collaborations. The vertical axis is density. The solid line in the figure represents the K-density, and the dashed lines represent the global confidence bands. (Source: [10])

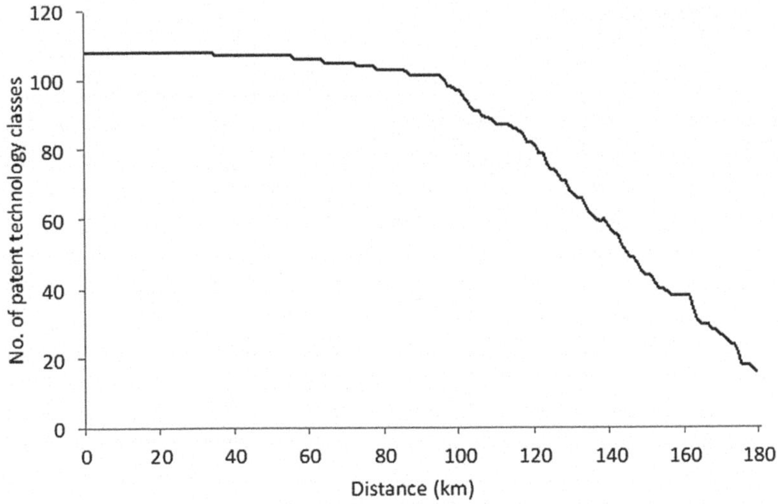

Fig. 5.2 Number of localized technology classes for each distance. (Source: [10])

Table 5.2 Frequency distributions of Γ. (Source: [10])

Range of Γ	Number of technology classes
0	12
0–0.1	21
0.1–0.2	48
0.2–0.3	30
0.3–0.4	8
0.4–0.5	1

5.5 Temporal Analysis

By sorting the data with respect to time and separating it by periods, we can observe how localization changes. Localization measured by patent citations declines over time [7]. Therefore, distance frictions in codified knowledge spillovers are disappearing. Since the period of analysis (1986–2005) was characterized by vast developments in ICT and a dramatic decrease in communication costs, we would expect a reduction in collaboration costs between geographically remote establishments. However, this is not the case for collaboration.

To investigate periodic changes in the localization tendency, the data are separated into 5-year periods. Potential collaborators are also separated in each period.

Figure 5.3 depicts the results. Panels (a), (b), (c), and (d) show the results for 1986–1990, 1991–1995, 1996–2000, and 2001–2005, respectively. The shapes of the K-densities are mostly stable. Furthermore, the estimated values of Γ are 0.205, 0.216, 0.243, and 0.249 for 1985–1990, 1991–1995 1996–2000, and 2001–2005, respectively. The extent of localization has an increasing rather than a decreasing

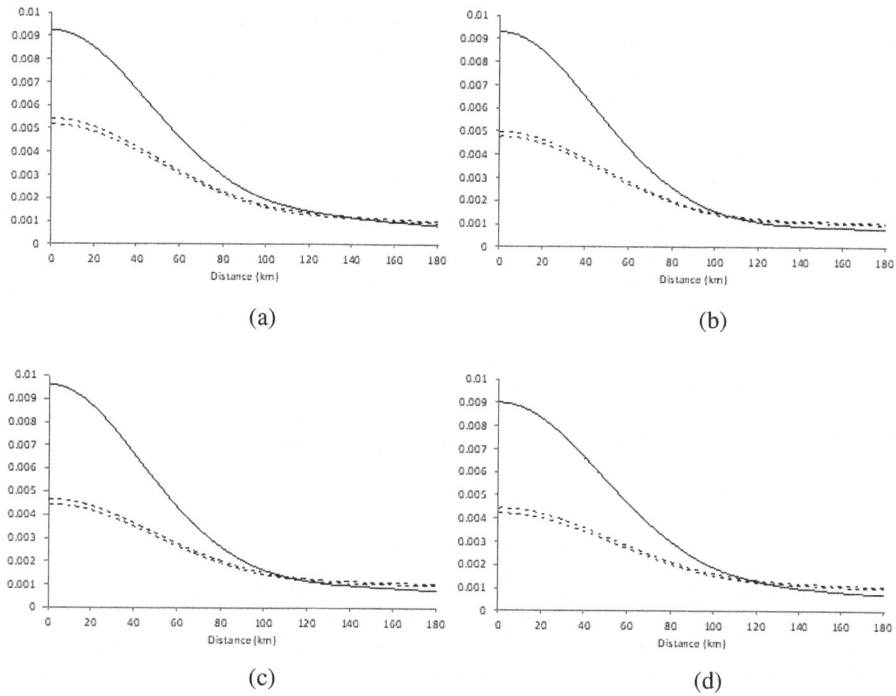

Fig. 5.3 Results weighted by establishment creativity. The vertical axes represent density. (Source: [10]). (**a**) 1986–1990. (**b**) 1991–1995. (**c**) 1996–2000. (**d**) 2001–2005

trend across these periods. This tendency implies that the geographic frictions in collaborations are unchanged or even increasing over time, which suggests the importance of geographical proximity in the exchange of tacit knowledge that requires face-to-face communication.

The literature indicates that tacit knowledge transfer requires high communication costs and has large geographic impediments based on evidence from the geographic distribution of multinational firms' operations [12].

5.6 Firm-Border Effects

As indicated in the literature, firm-border effects may significantly impede collaborations because the fear of leakage necessitates additional management costs in inter-firm collaboration [17]. To capture the firm-border effect, the data are divided into two groups: intra-firm collaborations and inter-firm collaborations. Intra-firm collaborations are collaborations between establishments that belong to the same firm, whereas inter-firm collaborations are collaborations between establishments that belong to different firms. We then examine the localization of collaboration in the two groups and compare them.

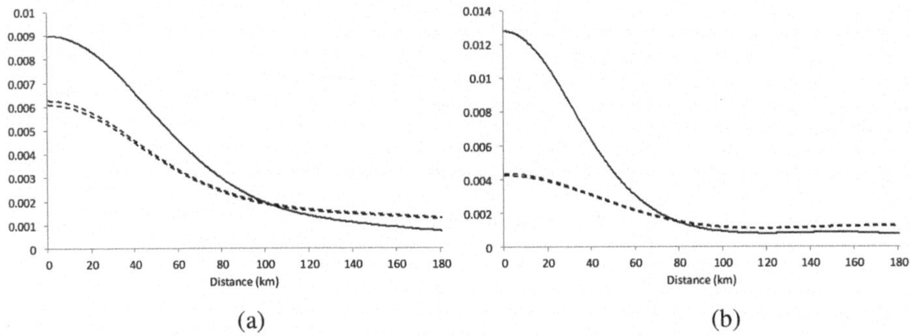

Fig. 5.4 K-densities and confidence bands of intra- and inter-firm collaborations. The vertical axes represent density. (Source: [10]). (**a**) Intra-firm collaborations. (**b**) Inter-firm collaborations

Since potential collaboration differs between inter- and intra-firm establishments, we need separate counterfactual collaborations for inter- and intra-firm collaborations. Counterfactual collaborations in the intra-firm case are chosen from among the establishments within a firm. Similarly, counterfactual inter-firm collaborations are chosen from among establishments that belong to different firms.

Figure 5.4 depicts the results. Panel (a) shows the K-density and global confidence bands of intra-firm collaborations. The actual K-density is above the upper global confidence band for every distance in the 0–100 km range. Panel (b) shows the K-density and global confidence bands of the inter-firm collaborations. The K-density is above the upper global confidence band for every distance in the 0–77 km range.

Regarding the degree of localization, the estimated values of Γ are 0.155 and 0.300 for intra- and inter-firm collaboration, respectively. This estimate means that inter-firm collaboration is more localized than intra-firm collaboration.

Such an inter- vs intra-firm comparison can be conducted in a technology-by-technology analysis. Figure 5.5 depicts the number of technology classes that are localized at each distance. We observe a clear difference between intra- and inter-firm collaborations. Although 99 of the 120 technology classes are localized in inter-firm collaborations, only approximately 62 technology classes are localized in intra-firm collaborations. Furthermore, the number of localized industries in inter-firm collaborations is lower at shorter distances (approximately 80 km).

Table 5.3 reports the frequency distributions of Γ in intra- and inter-firm collaborations. Of the 120 technology classes, 19 are not localized in inter-firm collaboration (Γ equals 0), while the corresponding number for intra-firm collaboration is 42. The results suggest that more technology classes exhibit localization in inter-firm collaboration than in intra-firm collaboration.

The comparison between inter-firm and intra-firm collaboration shows that they have different degrees of localization and that localization is stronger in inter-firm collaborations. Therefore, the firm-border effect in collaboration is likely counterbalanced by geographic proximity. Concretely, collaborations between firms

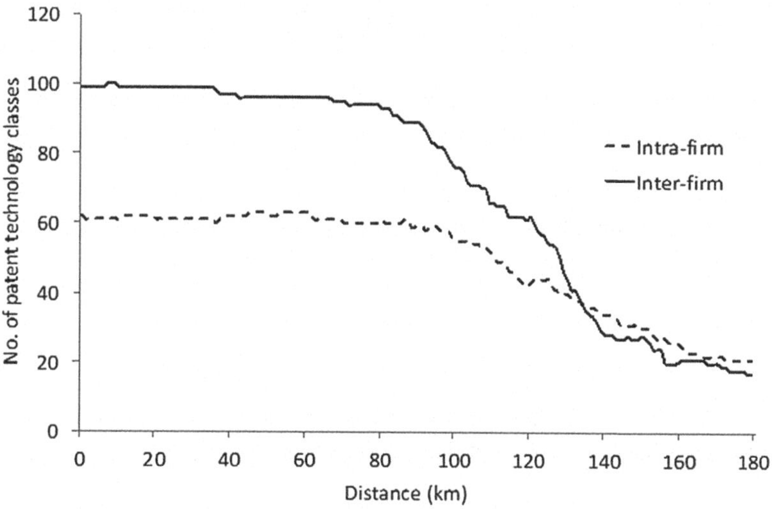

Fig. 5.5 Number of localized technology classes at each distance (intra- compared with inter-firm). The dashed line represents intra-firm collaborations, and the solid line represents inter-firm collaborations. (Source: [10])

Table 5.3 Frequency distributions of Γ, intra- and inter-firm collaboration. (Source: [10])

Range of Γ	Intra-firm	Inter-firm
0	42	19
0–0.1	45	32
0.1–0.2	23	39
0.2–0,3	7	19
0.3–0.4	2	9
0.4–0.5	0	2
0.5–0.6	0	0
0.6–0.7	1	0

are intuitively more difficult that those within firms because interests conflict and unwanted transfers of knowledge and organizational secrets significantly harm firm competitiveness [8, 17]. Moreover, the literature indicates that geographic proximity facilitates monitoring firms' private information in venture capital investment and credit lending relations between small firms and banks [1, 14].

To confirm the role of geographic proximity, the author and the co-author on the original paper on which this chapter is based conducted interviews in March 2016 with firms that have experience in collaborative projects in a provincial but industrial city in Nagano Prefecture in Japan. The managers of these firms mentioned that geographical proximity promotes trust between firms through monitoring and spillovers of each firm's information and facilitates collaboration between firms.

5.7 Firm Size Effect on Inter-firm Collaboration

This section further discusses the firm-border effect. The firm-border effect may differ with respect to firm size. To examine the firm size effect, the sample is divided into multiple-establishment firms and single-establishment firms. Multiple-establishment firms can be regarded as large firms, and single-establishment firms can be regarded as small firms. Multiple- and single-establishment firms are defined according to the number of establishments that have applied for patents in the data. Thus, if establishments did not apply for patents in the period from 1986 to 2005, they cannot be identified. Figure 5.6 depicts the results. The panels in Fig. 5.6 represent the K-density and global confidence bands in each type of collaboration (single–single, multiple–multiple, and multiple–single). In every panel from (a) to (c), the K-densities are above the upper confidence bands at shorter distances; therefore, the collaboration is significantly localized in every case.

The estimated values of Γ are 0.334, 0.253, and 0.330 for single–single, multiple–multiple, and multiple–single collaborations, respectively. Interestingly, Γ is higher for small firms, which suggests that small firms are more sensitive to collaboration distance.

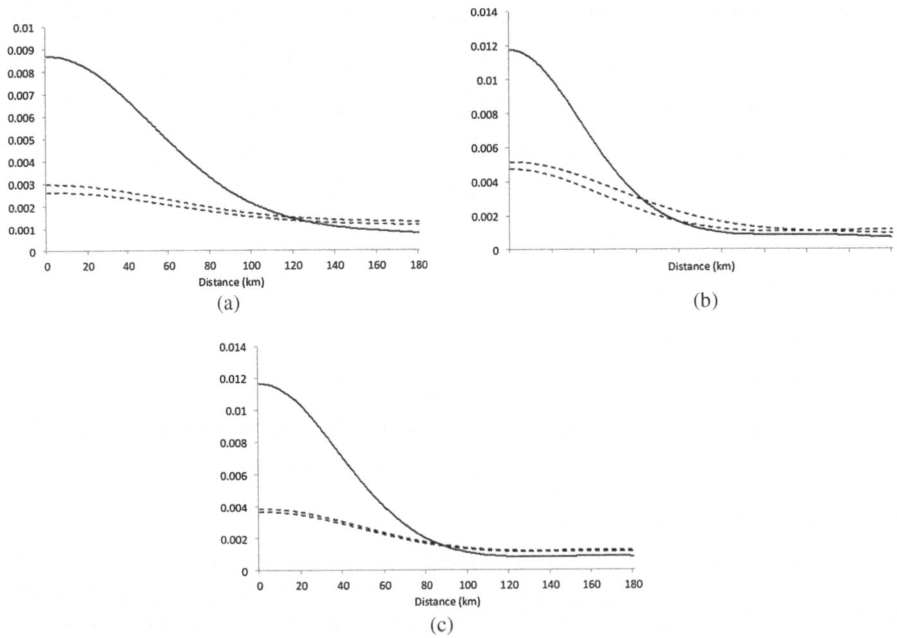

Fig. 5.6 K-densities and firm size effects in inter-firm collaborations. The vertical axes represent density. The meanings of the lines are the same as in the previous figures. (Source: [10]). (**a**) Single-single collaborations. (**b**) Multiple-multiple collaborations. (**c**) Multiple-single collaborations

5.8 Discussion

This chapter investigated the localization of establishment-level collaborations recorded in patent data. The findings in this chapter are summarized as follows. First, collaborations between establishments are significantly localized at the 5% level with a localization range of approximately 100 km. Second, localization in collaboration is observed for most technology categories. Third, the extent of such localization remained stable over the course of two decades (1986–2005). Fourth, the extent of localization is substantially larger in inter-firm than in intra-firm collaboration. Finally, in inter-firm collaboration, the extent of localization is larger when small firms are involved.

The finding that the localization of collaboration remained stable over the course of two decades provides a new perspective on the differences in geographic frictions between collaboration and knowledge spillovers. The frictions in knowledge spillovers observed in patent citations decline over time [7]. This difference between collaborations and patent citations may indicate that ICT may not fully compensate for the geographic frictions involved when face-to-face communication is required.

Moreover, this chapter reports quantitative evidence on the firm-border effect in collaborations, which has long been a subject of debate [8, 17]. The greater localization observed for inter- relative to with intra-firm collaborations suggests that the collaboration between different firms entails additional managerial costs due to the fear of unwanted knowledge transfer and leaked organizational secrets in inter-firm collaborations. This indicates that geographic proximity encourages trust between firms and reduces monitoring costs.

Although localized knowledge spillovers have been the theoretical basis for cluster policy, it is also true that distance may no longer matter because of the vast development of ICT. However, this chapter demonstrates that geographically localized knowledge spillovers between establishments remain crucial for innovation. Thus, promoting the location of businesses within a proximate distance through policy can facilitate research collaborations.

References

1. Agarwal S, Hauswald R. Distance and private information in lending. Rev Financ Stud. 2010;23(7):2757–88.
2. Arbia G, Espa G, Quah D. A class of spatial econometric methods in the empirical analysis of clusters of firms in the space. Empir Econ. 2008;34(1):81–103.
3. Cairncross F. The death of distance: how the communications revolution is changing our lives. Boston: Harvard Business School Press; 2001. ISBN: 9781578514380.
4. Carlino GA, et al. The agglomeration of R&D labs. Working Paper Series 12–22. Federal Reserve Bank of Philadelphia; 2012.
5. Duranton G, Overman HG. Testing for localization using micro-geographic data. Rev Econ Stud. 2005;72(4):1077–106.

6. Goto A, Motohashi K. Construction of a Japanese patent database and a first look at Japanese patenting activities. Res Policy. 2007;36(9):1431–42.
7. Griffith R, Lee S, Van Reenen J. Is distance dying at last? Falling home bias in fixed-effects models of patent citations. Quant Econ. 2011;2(2):211–49.
8. Hausler J, Hohn H-W, Lutz S, et al. Contingencies of innovative networks: a case study of successful interfirm R&D collaboration. Res Policy. 1994;23(1):47–66.
9. Inoue H, Nakajima K, Saito Y. Localization of knowledge-creating establishments. Jpn World Econ. 2017;43:23–9.
10. Inoue H, Nakajima K, Saito Y. Localization of collaborations in knowledge creation. Ann Reg Sci. 2019;62(1):119–40.
11. Jaffe AB, Trajtenberg M, Henderson R. Geographic localization of knowledge spillovers as evidenced by patent citations. Q J Econ. 1993;108:577–98.
12. Keller W, Yeaple SR. The gravity of knowledge. Am Econ Rev. 2013;103(4):1414–44.
13. Kerr WR, Kominers SD. Agglomerative forces and cluster shapes. Rev Econ Stat. 2015;97(4):877–99.
14. Lerner J. Venture capitalists and the oversight of private firms. J Financ. 1995;50(1):301–18.
15. Murata Y, et al. Localized knowledge spillovers and patent citations: a distance-based approach. Rev Econ Stat. 2014;96(5):967–85.
16. OECD. Compendium of patent statistics. Technical report. Paris: OECD; 2008.
17. Pittaway L, et al. Networking and innovation: a systematic review of the evidence. Int J Manag Rev. 2004;5(3–4):137–68.
18. Saito YU, Yamauchi I. Inventors' mobility and organizations' productivity: evidence from Japanese rare name inventors. RIETI Discussion Paper Series, 15-E-128; 2015.
19. Suzuki J. The structural characteristics of research and development by Japanese companies, and issues for the future. RIETI Discussion Paper Series, 11-J-002; 2011.
20. Thompson P, Fox-Kean M. Patent citations and the geography of knowledge spillovers: a reassessment. Am Econ Rev. 2005;95(1):450–60.

Chapter 6
Community of Establishment Networks

6.1 Introduction

Chapter 5 examines how bilateral collaborations between establishments are connected, especially regarding distance distributions. However, when we merely consider individual collaborations or interactions in isolation, we cannot understand the complex nature of the system. This is because, for example, a connection with a node that has many links with other nodes and a connection with a node that has no previous links have completely different values. If we apply this logic to the example of human friendships, it becomes easy to understand. Therefore, in this chapter, to grasp the complex nature of collaborations between establishments, we discuss their community structure. A community is a densely connected network structure, and identifying communities enables us to understand what establishments exchange dense information among one another, rather than as a bilateral relationship. This chapter is based on the author's prior paper [13]. Figures and tables are replicated with proper permission from the publisher. The main text is modified to fit the context of this book.

As noted above, Chap. 5 revealed how geographical frictions are related to existence of links between establishments [14] in the form of bilateral relationships. However, knowledge can be propagated to indirectly connected firms through firms with direct connections, as is widely discussed in the literature [5–7, 9, 10]. Therefore, we should consider a more complex structure than bilateral relationships. In other words, we should consider a network of firms and examine densely connected components of it, i.e. communities. The community is a potent unit of knowledge propagation. In line with Chap. 5, we examine establishments.

This chapter investigates the significant characteristics of communities detected through a collaborative network. Specifically, four metrics are discussed. The first is the similarity in the total number of patents, which can be considered a quantitative proxy for knowledge-creation experience. Establishments with less experience may

H. Inoue, *Co-patenting: An Analytic Tool for Cooperative Research and Development*, Evolutionary Economics and Social Complexity Science 21,
https://doi.org/10.1007/978-4-431-54807-2_6

want to be connected with experienced establishments, or conversely, similarly experienced establishments may tend to be connected. The second metric is the similarity in the total number of patent citations, which can be considered a qualitative proxy for knowledge-creation experience. As in the case of the quantitative measure, either homophily or heterophily may be found. The third metric is knowledge similarity. If establishments have totally different knowledge bases, it will be difficult for them to collaborate. Therefore, establishments with similar knowledge would be in the same community. However, as the literature shows [3], if most of the knowledge held by firms is the same, they will be less likely to create new ideas. Therefore, it is not appropriate to predict the results for this metric. The fourth metric is geographic proximity. We address this issue in the context of bilateral relationships in Chap. 5, and no previous study has demonstrated its significance for communities, which we do here.

6.2 Data

This chapter also uses the establishment-level collaboration data set based on the Institute of Intellectual Property (IIP) patent database [11]. From this database, we select patents with an application date between 1993 and 2008. After identifying the establishments, collaborations between them are also identified.

In this chapter, we need to have a network of establishments. If a patent includes more than one establishment, links are drawn pairwise between all establishments. In this process, duplicate links are ignored to generate an unweighted network, and duplicates are employed to create a weighted network.

An overview of the database is provided in Table 6.1. The patent data obtained from IIP include 12,387,628 patents. Establishments applied for 7,392,306 of these patents. As the data on establishment patents show, collaborative patents are a minority of the total, but at 466,329, the number is sufficient for our analysis. From a network perspective, there are 58,122 establishments that serve as nodes and 142,086 collaborations that serve as links.

As one of the four properties, we consider the geographic distance between collaborating establishments. As mentioned above, the locations of the establishments are identified. Then, the distance is calculated for all combinations of paired establishments in a given community, and we obtain the average for the community.

Table 6.1 Number of observations obtained from patents. (Source: [13])

No. of patents	12,387,628
No. of patents applied for by establishments	7,392,206
No. of patents applied for by collaborations of establishments	466,329
No. of establishments (nodes)	58,122
No. of collaborations between establishments (links)	142,086

We need to obtain the lengths of the knowledge vectors. First, a knowledge vector is created for each establishment through its history of patent applications. The dimensions of the vector are based on the number of technology classes of its patents. Here, the International Patent Classification is used: since there are 129 classes, the vector has 129 dimensions. The elements of a knowledge vector represent the number of patents in each technology class [2]. Second, the knowledge distance is obtained between collaborating establishments using the Mahalanobis distance [4]. After the distances of all combinations for a given community are calculated, we obtain the average for the community.

6.3 Community Detection

As defined previously, nodes in a given community are densely connected to one another but not to outside communities. Extracting communities is helpful because it offers us a coarse-grained view of the network. Therefore, extracting communities has attracted broad academic interest, and several methods for doing so have been developed. One highly evaluated approach is the map equation method [18], which outperforms other methods in community extraction [1, 16].

The map equation method uses random walkers and information theory. The name "map equation" derives from the following equation:

$$L(C) = q_{\curvearrowright} H(C) + \sum_{i=1}^{m} p_{\circlearrowright}^{i} H(\mathcal{P}^{i}), \tag{6.1}$$

where $L(C)$ measures the average description length when a random walker migrates through links between the nodes of a network with a given set of communities. The right-hand side consists of two parts. The first term reflects movements of the random walker across communities. $q_{\curvearrowright}$ is the probability that the random walker switches communities, and $H(C)$ is the average description length of the community index given by its Shannon entropy. The second term reflects movements of the random walker within communities. $p_{\circlearrowright}^{i}$ is the fraction of the movements within community i, and $H(\mathcal{P}^{i})$ is the entropy of code in community i.

A random walker will remain in a densely connected area of the network for a relatively long time. Therefore, if the index for communities and frequently visited nodes is short, the length $L(C)$ will be shorter.

The above map equation considers one-layered communities. However, detecting hierarchical communities is a natural extension, and thus, the method has been enhanced to search recursively for communities [19].

Table 6.2 lists the results of the community detection process. There are two sets of results. One is for the unweighted network that ignores duplication. The other is for the weighted network, i.e. the weight is the duplication count. Layers of communities are detected recursively, and a given establishment belongs to only

Table 6.2 Community detection and results: unweighted and weighted. Since communities are recursively detected, layers are shown. The numbers in the "Communities" row indicate how many communities are found in a given layer. The numbers in the "Leaf nodes" row indicate how many establishments are not assigned to communities. (Source: [13])

Unweighted					
Layers	1	2	3	4	
Communities	3,967	2,591	960	0	
Leaf nodes	0	8,961	43,603	5,558	
Weighted					
Layers	1	2	3	4	5
Communities	3,997	3,198	941	2	0
Leaf nodes	0	8,960	41,885	7,272	5

one community at some layer. The numbers in the "Communities" row in each table indicate how many communities are found in the layer in question. The numbers in the "Leaf nodes" row in each table indicate how many establishments are not assigned to communities in the layer, meaning that no community is detected for those establishments.

Although weighted and unweighted networks can be obtained, there is no criterion for determining which is better, and it may depend on the purpose at hand. However, since we can incorporate the strength of connections between nodes when using the weighted network, we employ it hereafter. The table shows that if up to the first and second communities are considered, most leaf nodes are included in those two layers. Note that the leaf nodes in the third layer are the nodes assigned to the second layer. Therefore, these two layers are considered hereafter.

Figure 6.1 shows the distribution of the community sizes: The top panel shows the first layer, and the bottom shows the second layer. Here, community size means the number of total establishments included in a community. A high concentration of establishments is observed in the largest community in the first layer. In contrast, a straight line is observed for the second line in the log-log plots, which means a fat-tailed distribution.

The distributions reveal that there are communities of different sizes. It is necessary to determine what size is an appropriate minimum for a community because it does not seem appropriate to treat one or a few establishments as communities and compare them to other, larger communities. However, there is no decisive criterion for minimum community size. For the analysis to make practical sense, the communities from the second layer that have at least ten establishments are extracted. In addition, if a community from the first layer does not have a second layer, that community is extracted if the size is 10 or more. As a result, 1,046 communities are extracted consisting of 40,312 nodes.

Since community detection is used, one might argue that it is advisable to identify the resolution limit of the community detection process. Indeed, the selection of the resolution limit should be made with caution in modularity optimization methods [8]. However, mainly because Infomap is a hierarchical method, the resolution limit can be ignored [15].

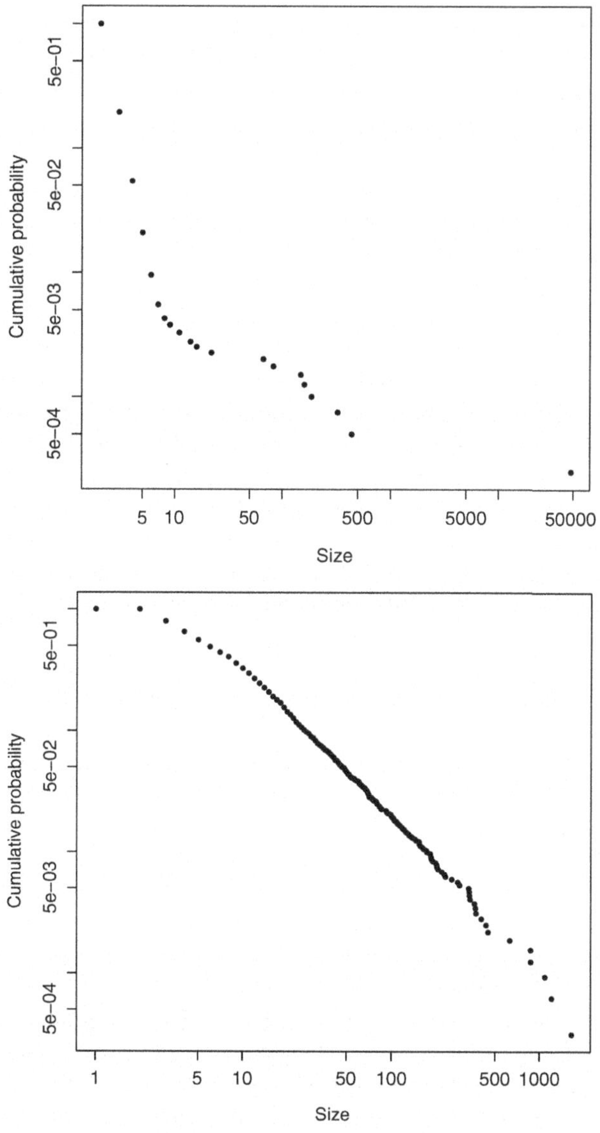

Fig. 6.1 Community size distributions of the first and second layers: the top panel is for the first layer, and the bottom panel is for the second. The horizontal axes show the number of establishments included in each community. The vertical axes show the complementary cumulative probability. (Source: [13])

6.4 Results

This chapter discusses the four properties of communities: the number of patents, the patent citations, the geographical distance, and the length of the knowledge vector.

The number of patents is a quantitative proxy for innovation capability. To examine the proximity of the number of patents in a community we use the standard deviation. One could argue that the distribution of the number of patents in communities should be a bell curve for the standard deviation to be used and not be highly skewed. However, since the standard deviation is the most straightforward statistic for determining variation, this metric is used to capture proximity. If it is small, the community exhibits homophily in its quantitative capability.

The number of patent citations is a qualitative proxy for innovation capability. The number of citations for which an establishment applied is tallied. Note that a citation is normalized by the average number of citations in the same year because older patents are more likely to be cited. As with the number of patents, we analyse whether establishments in a given community have a similar number of citations. Therefore, we calculate the standard deviation of the total number of citations in a community. If it is small, the community exhibits homophily in qualitative capability.

Although citations are broadly used as a proxy of patent quality [12, 17, 20], note that all citations are not equal and that they are affected by various issues, such as self-citations and defensive patents. However, there is no decisive methodology to adjust citations. Therefore, citations are simply adjusted by year as discussed above.

Geographical distance is a proxy for communication costs. Establishments in a community may locate near one another to communicate at a lower cost. However, if recent advances in information communication technology reduce the cost of communication, we may not obtain significant results for geographical distance. The geodesic distance is calculated for all combinations of establishments in a community, and the average is obtained. The hypothesis is that a short distance is significant for the community.

Finally, the length of the knowledge vector is analysed. If establishments want to incorporate knowledge from outside establishments, there should be some knowledge distance between them. However, if they have totally different technologies, they will have no opportunity to collaborate. Thus, these are opposing hypotheses. As with the geographical distance, we calculate the knowledge distance for all combinations of establishments in a community and obtain the average.

Randomized data are created to validate the significance of these properties in actual communities. For the randomized data, we create 10,000 communities, and each community size is chosen from the actual distribution of community size. By contrast, as shown in the previous section, the actual data have 1,046 communities containing 40,312 establishments in total.

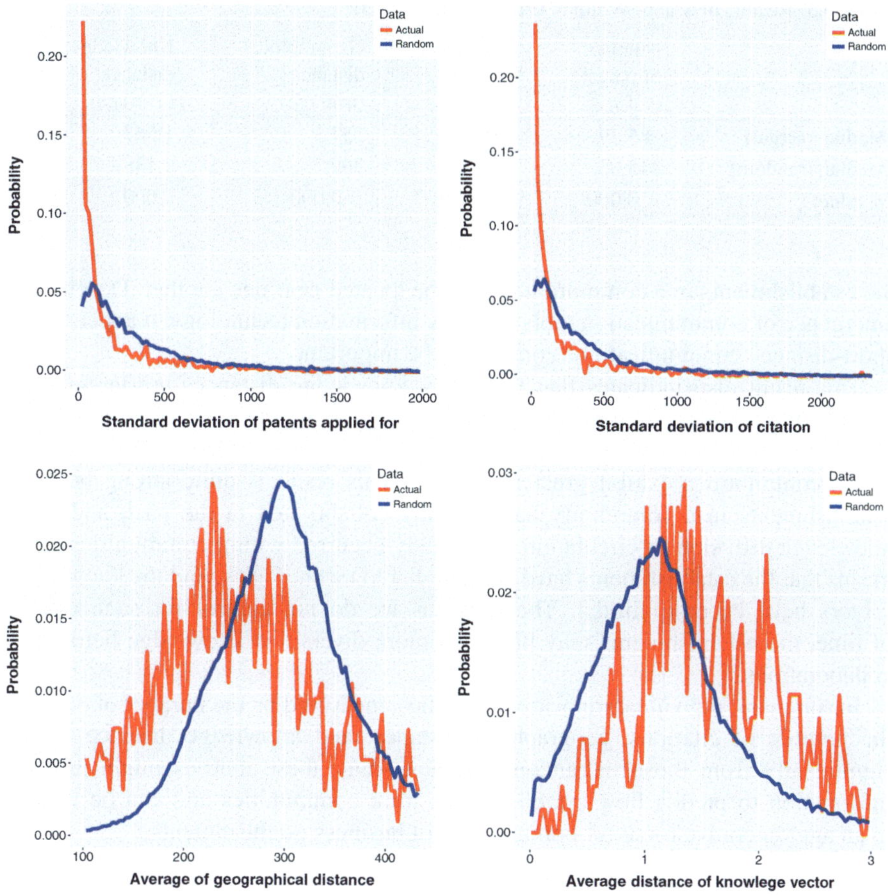

Fig. 6.2 Results for four properties: The top-left panel is for the number of patents; the top-right panel is for citations; the bottom-left panel is for geographical distance; and the bottom-right panel is for knowledge vectors. (Source: [13])

Figure 6.2 shows the results for the four properties. As we can see in the top two panels, i.e. the number of patents and citations, the actual data tend to have smaller standard deviations than the random data. In addition, we also observe clear differences between the bottom two panels, which represent geographical distance and knowledge distance.

Table 6.3 reports the test results. To avoid making assumptions for the distributions, we employ the Mann–Whitney U test. The actual number of patents and number of citations are significantly smaller than those in the random data. Therefore, establishments in communities exhibit similarity in these two metrics.

The result for geographical distance is also significant. We find that the distance between establishments in communities is short, and this result is significant. The bilateral distance involved in collaborations is short [14], and this result shows that

Table 6.3 Results of Mann–Whitney U tests. (Source: [13])

	Number of patent (s.d.)	Citations (s.d.)	Geographical distance (average)	Knowledge distance (average)
Median (actual)	85.29	85.14	257.3	1.567
Median (random)	245.05	244.15	309.7	1.138
p value	0.000	0.000	0.000	0.000

the establishments in a community tend to be located near one another. Despite the emergence of communication tools aided by information technology, it appears that short-distance communications continue to be important.

This result also indicates that the actual knowledge distances are larger than those in the randomized data. One could expect that a community with randomly chosen establishments would have a greater diversity of knowledge. However, the actual communities exhibit greater diversity. This result is quite strong because establishments in a community have already collaborated in the past, and thus, knowledge diffusion or circulation has already occurred within communities. This means that the establishments have already shared technologies, and the knowledge vectors have become similar. Therefore, as we do not control for such effects of time, the establishments may have had more diversified knowledge before the collaborations.

In summary, individual innovative activities, measured by the number of patents, the number of citations, geographical distance, and knowledge distance, differ significantly from those in random samples. Thus, these metrics might provide information to predict how establishments form communities and can be related to an agglomerative force for communities of business establishments.

6.5 Discussion

This chapter discussed what metrics are related to agglomeration for knowledge-creating establishments. By using unique Japanese patent data and Infomap, which is a proven method of community detection, Japanese establishments are separated into communities based on connections through joint patent applications. Comparing the actual and random communities reveals the following facts. (1) The numbers of patents applied for tend to be similar in a community: This means that establishments in a community have similar abilities in terms of the quantity of innovation. (2) The total numbers of citations also tend to be similar: This means that establishments in a community have similar ability in terms of the quality of innovation. (3) The geographic distance is significantly small: Actual communities tend to be located near one another. (4) The knowledge distance is significantly large: Establishments in actual communities have greater knowledge distance than those in randomly created communities. In short, the establishments are similar in the patent output and citations they generate, are located near one another, and differ in the knowledge dimension.

In this chapter, we saw how establishments behave collectively. The literature discusses bilateral relationships but not communities. For example, Chaps. 4 and 5 discussed the locations of establishments. Since agglomerative forces other than distance are found in this chapter, this work complements the literature on forces of agglomeration.

We have avoided discussing the causal relations between communities and our metrics because of the presence of endogeneity. An establishment is a component of a community. This means that the establishment affects the other components while simultaneously be affected by the other components. To discuss this issue, we should consider how a network grows over time if such relationships affect growth. To answer this question, the following chapters discuss generative network models.

References

1. Barabási A-L. Network science. Cambridge: Cambridge University Press; 2016.
2. Benner M, Waldfogel. J. Close to you? Bias and precision in patent-based measures of technological proximity. Res Policy. 2008;37(9):1556–67.
3. Berliant M, Fujita M. Knowledge creation as a square dance on the Hilbert cube. Int Econ Rev. 2008;49(4):1251–95.
4. Bloom NN, Schankerman M, Van Reenen J. Identifying technology spillovers and product market rivalry. Econometrica. 2013;81(4):1347–93.
5. Fleming L, King III C, Juda AI. Small worlds and regional innovation. Organ Sci. 2007;18(6):938–54.
6. Fleming L, Mingo S, Chen D. Collaborative brokerage, generative creativity, and creative success. Admin Sci Q. 2007;52(3):443–75.
7. Forti E, Franzoni C, Sobrero M. Bridges or isolates? Investigating the social networks of academic inventors. Res Policy. 2013;42(8):1378–88.
8. Fortunato S, Barthelemy M. Resolution limit in community detection. Proc Natl Acad Sci. 2007;104(1):36–41.
9. Gautam A. Collaboration networks, structural holes, and innovation: a longitudinal study. Admin Sci Q. 2000;45(3):425–55.
10. Gonzalez-Brambila CN, Veloso FM, Krackhardt D. The impact of network embeddedness on research output. Res Pol. 2013;42(9):1555–67.
11. Goto A, Motohashi K. Construction of a Japanese patent database and a first look at Japanese patenting activities. Res Policy. 2007;36(9):1431–42.
12. Griliches Z. R&D and productivity-the economic evidence. Chicago: The University of Chicago Press; 1998.
13. Inoue H. The community structure of business establishments and its properties: evidence from joint patent applications. Evol Inst Econ Rev. 2018;15(2):465–75.
14. Inoue H, Nakajima K, Saito Y. Localization of collaborations in knowledge creation. Ann Reg Sci. 2019;62(1):119–40.
15. Kawamoto T, Rosvall M. Estimating the resolution limit of the map equation in community detection. Phys Rev E. 2015;91(1):012809.
16. Lancichinetti A, Fortunato S. Community detection algorithms: a comparative analysis. Phys Rev E. 2009;80(5):056117.

17. Nagaoka S, Motohashi K, Goto A. Patent statistics as an innovation indicator. In: Hall BH, editor. Handbook of the economics of innovation, vol. 2. Amsterdam: Elsevier; 2010. p. 1083–127.
18. Rosvall M, Bergstrom CT. Maps of random walks on complex networks reveal community structure. Proc Natl Acad Sci. 2008;105(4):1118–23.
19. Rosvall M, Bergstrom CT. Multilevel compression of random walks on networks reveals hierarchical organization in large integrated systems. PloS One. 2011;6(4):e18209.
20. Trajtenberg M. A penny for your quotes: patent citations and the value of innovations. Rand J Econ. 21(1);1990:172–87.

Chapter 7
Generative Model: Distance and Past Connection

7.1 Introduction

The previous chapters examined the bilateral relationships of actors and communities in a network. These empirical results help us to understand the behaviour of actors but not the evolution of this behaviour over time. Understanding such development is important for each actor's efforts to develop a collaboration strategy and for the government to craft innovation policies. The present chapter discusses a model of the evolution of this behaviour, which is based on [6]. Figures and tables are replicated with proper permission from the publisher. The main text is modified to fit the context of this book.

This chapter discusses the structure and a generative model of establishments' co-patenting networks. Their structure has been described in Chap. 2. The present chapter examines additional structural facts and introduces a model to replicate the network. Japanese patent data are used for the analyses in this chapter.

Since our focus is on the network and the links in it, this chapter assesses the extent to which the proposed model can replicate the network's degree distribution. Numerous mechanisms could drive the evolution of network links, as we saw in Chap. 6. In network science, however, it is well known that the likelihood of a node acquiring a new link is proportional to the links the node has acquired in the past [2]. This kind of relational expression cannot be analysed using conventional approaches such as multiple linear regression analysis. This is why we need to use a growth model.

In addition, the model in this chapter also considers geographical relevance in the relations among nodes. Concretely, when the growth model begins creating links, the nodes in the original geographic positions are used. By using their original geographic positions, the model considers the degree of and distance between nodes and chooses which links between nodes should be added.

H. Inoue, *Co-patenting: An Analytic Tool for Cooperative Research and Development*, Evolutionary Economics and Social Complexity Science 21,
https://doi.org/10.1007/978-4-431-54807-2_7

7.2 Analyses of the Joint Application Network

Although the approach to using patent data is exactly the same as in previous chapters, the database on which this chapter is based is different and was prepared by Tamada et al. [10]. It includes 4,998,464 patents published in patent gazettes from January 1993 to December 2002.

Table 7.1 summarizes the counts. Table 7.1 reports the numbers of nodes and links. If we distinguish between head offices and branch offices, there are 54,197 nodes and 154,205 links. If we do not distinguish between these two types of offices, there are 24,767 nodes and 105,088 links. There are 2.19 times more nodes and 1.47 times more links in the former case, and hence, the gaps between the figures are substantial. For the remainder of the chapter, head and branch offices, i.e. establishments, are used.

Figure 7.1 plots the various distributions for the joint application network. Figure 7.1a shows the degree distribution. The horizontal axis represents the degree, and the vertical axis shows the rank. The figures are plotted on logarithmic scales. Rank representations are used for the distributions because we can directly understand the forms of a cumulative probability.

The cumulative probability of the degree distribution appears to be linear. If it can be fitted to a line, it might follow a power law. It is important to determine whether the degree distribution follows a power law because we can then make judgments about whether we can use the previously published growth model that follows a power law.

Generally, the least-squares method is used for verification, and the inclination (the power index) of the power-law distribution is estimated. However, this approach has two critical flaws. The first is that people cannot determine whether a distribution really follows a power law. (With this method, the inclination can be estimated for any kind of distribution.) The second is that people cannot determine which part of the distribution follows a power law.

Clauset et al. [4] created a method that combines maximum-likelihood fitting methods with goodness-of-fit tests based on the Kolmogorov-Smirnov statistic. This method was novel because it was the first to solve the above problems.

The degree is discrete, and the power law distribution for a discrete case is defined as follows:

$$p(x) = \frac{x^{-\alpha}}{\zeta(\alpha, x_{\min})}, \tag{7.1}$$

Table 7.1 Number of nodes and links in the joint application network. (Source: [6])

Use of inventors' addresses	Used (head and branch offices)	Not used (head offices only)
Number of nodes	54,197	24,767
Number of links	154,205	105,088

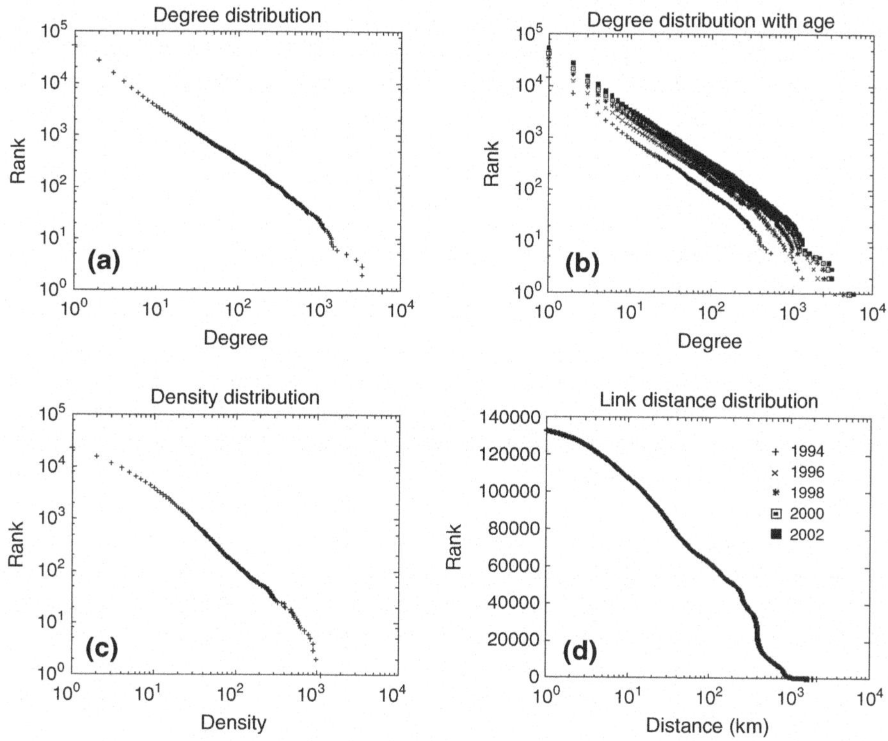

Fig. 7.1 Distribution data. (**a**) is the degree distribution from 1993 to 2002. (**b**) is the degree distribution from 1993 to the indicated years. (**c**) is the density distribution. (**d**) is the link distance distribution. The vertical axis scale is linear in this graph. (Source: [6])

where

$$\zeta(\alpha, x_{\min}) = \sum_{n=0}^{\infty}(n + x_{\min})^{-\alpha}, \tag{7.2}$$

$x_{\min}$ is the lower bound, and α is the scaling parameter. $x_{\min}$ is necessary because $p(x)$ diverges at $x = 0$. For the cumulative distribution, the equation is defined as follows.

$$P(x) = \frac{\zeta(\alpha, x)}{\zeta(\alpha, x_{\min})}. \tag{7.3}$$

α is approximately calculated from $x_{\min}$ by the maximum likelihood estimator in the following equation:

$$\hat{\alpha} \simeq 1 + n\left[\sum_{i=1}^{n} \ln \frac{x_i}{x_{\min} - \frac{1}{2}}\right]^{-1}, \tag{7.4}$$

where $\hat{\alpha}$ is the estimated α.

The x_{min} is unknown and required. If the value is set, the distance between a model with the value and the actual cumulative probability can be calculated. One of the ways to calculate this distance is the Kolmogorov-Smirnov statistic, and the relevant equation is

$$D = \max_{x \geq x_{min}} |S(x) - P(x)|. \tag{7.5}$$

$S(x)$ is the cumulative distribution for the actual data, and $P(x)$ is the power law defined as (7.3) (with specific x_{min}).

The benchmark is necessary to determine whether D is small enough, i.e. whether the actual distribution plausibly follows a power law. A common approach is to use a goodness-of-fit test that generates a p-value that quantifies the plausibility of the hypothesis. In this test, distances between synthetic data sets and the model are created. The p-value is defined as the fraction of the synthetic distances that are larger than the actual distance. If p is large (close to 1), then the difference between the actual data and the model can be attributed to statistical noise alone; if it is small, the model is not plausibly fitted to the actual data. The literature regards $p > 0.1$ as a relatively conservative threshold.

A synthetic data set includes the same number of observations as the actual data, and these are randomly generated from the model with a specific x_{min}. The number of synthetic data sets is also important. Clauset et al. [4] use the following as a rule of thumb. "If we wish the p-value to be accurate to within approximately ϵ of the true value, we should generate about at least $\frac{1}{4}\epsilon^{-2}$." Here, it seems that using two decimal places is sufficient, so 2,500 synthetic data sets are created.

p-values are calculated in $1 \leq x_{min} \leq 10$. Figure 7.2 plots the results. As we can see, p is greater than 0.1 at $x_{min} \geq 7$. Hence, we can say that the cumulative distribution follows a power law, and the joint application network is a scale-free network. α is 2.03 at $x_{min} = 7$, for example. A range of degree exponents, more than -3 and less than -2, is observed in most networks [2]. Hence, the network's degree distribution is not unusual.

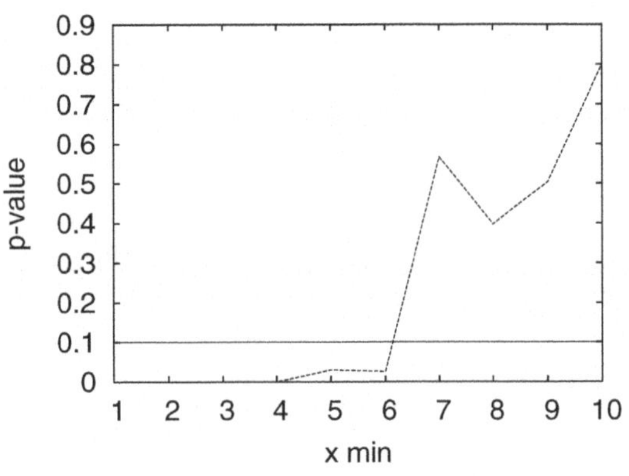

Fig. 7.2 Goodness-of-fit test. The horizontal axis represents the p-value. The vertical axis is x_{min}. The additional line depicts $p = 0.1$. (Source: [6])

Panel (b) in Fig. 7.1 also shows the degree distribution, but there are five different series of plots. These plots represent the degree distributions of networks with durations running from 1993 to the indicated years. The inclinations of these plots do not change as data are added.

Panel (c) in Fig. 7.1 plots the density distribution, which is calculated as the number of nodes within one square kilometre. The horizontal axis represents the node density, and the vertical axis represents the rank. They are on logarithmic scales. The distribution roughly follows a power law.

Panel (d) in Fig. 7.1 plots the distribution for the link distances. The horizontal axis depicts the link distance, and the vertical axis represents the rank. The horizontal axis is on a logarithmic scale, and distances of less than one kilometre have been dropped. The plot is nearly linear; thus, it seems that the probability distribution of the link distance is inversely related to the link distance. There are some peaks in the link distribution [5]. There is a peak at approximately 400 km and another at approximately 250 km. These distances correspond with those between Tokyo and Osaka and between Tokyo and Nagoya. These are large cities in Japan and are connected by efficient transportation infrastructure. This implies that link generation may be facilitated by travel time, not distance. Based on this assumption, we might obtain a smoother line on the graph if we place travel time, not geographic distance, on the horizontal axis.

7.3 A Growth Model and Verification

This section proposes a growth model to generate the same structure as the joint application network analysed in Sect. 7.2 and discusses its verification.

The preferential attachment model [1] is designed to generate scale-free networks and can be simply explained as follows.

1. A new node is incrementally added.
2. Links are placed between the new node and existing nodes. The probability Π of choosing an existing node is

$$\Pi(k_i) = k_i / \Sigma_i k_i,$$

   where k_i is the degree of the node.

The network generated by this model has a degree distribution that is expressed by $p(k) \propto k^{-3}$. This model does not take link distances into account. However, the model obviously should include link distance factors to show the structural features of distance. Therefore, one could minimally modify the preferential attachment model such that it includes distance factors [8, 9, 12]. This model has already been discussed and is suitable as the first step to investigate the geographic model for generating the joint application network. The algorithm is outlined below.

Algorithm for the modified preferential attachment model

1. Start with a complete graph consisting of m_0 nodes.
2. Add a node.
3. Append an address to it that is randomly chosen from the extracted establishments.
4. Add m links. Each link has a terminal of the node added in 2. A node for the other terminal of the link is chosen from existing nodes with probability

$$\Pi(k_j, d_{ij}) \propto k_j^{\alpha}/d_{ij}^{\sigma},$$

where i stands for the new node, j stands for the existing node(s), k_j is the degree of node j, and d_{ij} is the distance between nodes i and j. The distance between the nodes is calculated by the distance between two points on an ellipsoid, which is based on the latitude and longitude derived from the addresses of nodes. Finally, α and σ are constants. Duplications of links are prohibited.
5. Repeat steps (2)–(4) a fixed number of times.

In an earlier study [9], Manna and Sen investigated the case in which α was fixed to 1 in the above model They described the model's behaviour following variations in σ under the condition that the nodes were equally distributed within a square on a plane. Below, we will compare the results of the model described in the present chapter and that in this earlier study's model.

Other models can also generate scale-free networks. The fitness model [3] is representative of these, where each node has a weight, and if $w_i + w_j > \theta$, where w_i and w_j are weights of two arbitrary nodes, and θ is a constant, a link is stretched between them. Although this model has many advantages, it requires the researcher to define a threshold (θ). Therefore, to use this model, it is necessary to select a composite function of the distance and degree. The solution to this issue is unclear. On the other hand, the modified preferential attachment model is easier to evaluate because it only involves node degrees and link distances.

The rest of this section discusses how the model can reproduce the joint application network. To this end, various combinations of constants (α and σ) are considered and verify the results obtained with the original network with respect to the degree distribution and link distance distribution.

Figure 7.3 plots the simulation results. In the simulation, $m_0 = 3$, $m = 3$, and the final number of nodes is 3,000. Panels (a) and (b) of Fig. 7.3 depict the results under different α values. In other words, these results show the effects of the degree exponents on the probabilities of links. In these simulations, σ is fixed to 1.0.

Panel (a) of Fig. 7.3 plots the degree distribution. The axes are the same as those in the previous graphs of the degree distribution. The original network follows the power law (Panel (a) in Fig. 7.1); hence, $\alpha = 1$ indicates the closest result. Here, $\alpha = 0$ seems to be an exponential distribution, and $\alpha = 2$ has a few large degree nodes.

Panel (a) of Fig. 7.3 shows that the results demonstrate that there is a relationship between α and the degree distribution [7] described as follows: "When P_i grows

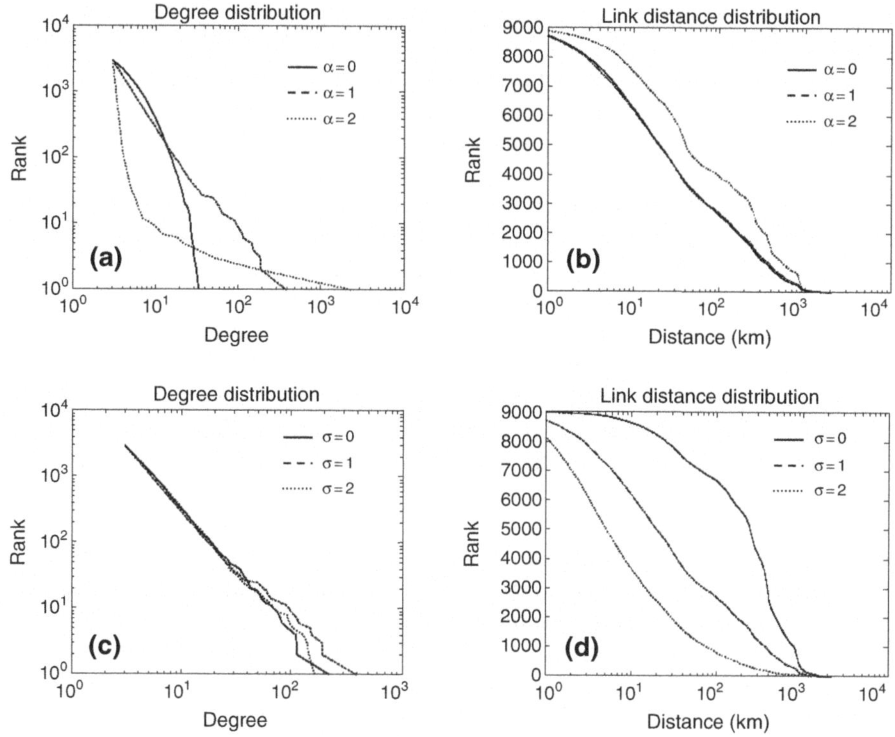

Fig. 7.3 Network data are generated by model. (**a**) depicts the degree distribution, and (**b**) represents the link distance distribution when $\alpha = 0$, 1 and 2, and $\sigma = 1$. (**c**) represents the degree distribution, and (**d**) is the link distance distribution when $\alpha = 1$ and $\sigma = 0$, 1 and 2. (Source: [6])

slower than linearly with k, the degree distribution decays faster than a power law in k. When P_i grows faster than linearly in k, a single node emerges that connects to nearly all other nodes." Since spatial effects are not considered in Krapivsky and Rendner's study, the relationship seems to be robust within some range of σ, and this is a topic deserving future study.

Panel (b) of Fig. 7.3 shows the link distance distribution. The axes are also the same as those in the previous graphs of the link distance distribution. The original network is in inverse proportion; hence, $\alpha = 0$ or 1 gives a closer result than $\alpha = 2$.

Panels (c) and (d) of Fig. 7.3 plot the results for different σ values. In other words, these results show the effects of the exponents of link distances in the probabilities of links. In these simulations, α is fixed to 1.0. Panel (c) of Fig. 7.3 plots the degree distribution. It is clear that $\sigma = 0$, 1, and 2 derive similar results. The effect of σ on the degree distribution seems to be small. Panel (d) of Fig. 7.3 plots the link distance distribution. Here, the link distance distribution depends on σ. $\sigma = 1$ achieves the closest results to the original network, $\sigma = 0$ has more long-distance links than the original network, and $\sigma = 2$ provides the opposite result. Since $\sigma = 0$ refers to the original preferential attachment model, this value is insufficient for reproducing the link distance.

These results demonstrate that α and σ substantially affect the structure of the network, and the best combination in this analysis is $\alpha = 1$ and $\sigma = 1$. However, we can study very little about the relationship between α and σ. This should be studied further in the future.

As mentioned above, this work considers the same model as Yook et al. [12]. Our best simulation result, $\alpha = 1$ and $\sigma = 1$, is the same as those for the Internet. The data (spatial distribution of nodes) used in the simulation are definitely different because one represents data from joint patent applications, and the other represents data from the Internet in North America. Therefore, this correspondence of the different data sets is interesting.

An earlier study reported that the link length distribution exponentially decays in the case of the Internet, i.e. it is proportional to $\exp(-l/l_0)$, where l_0 is a constant [11]. However, the results in the present work and Yook et al.'s study are different from that finding.

In Manna and Sen's study [9], α is fixed to 1 while σ varies. One of their results is that the link distance distribution is proportional to $l^{-\alpha+m-1}$ where m is a dimension. In the present work, α is 1 and m is 2; hence, the link distance distribution is constant. This conclusion differs from our simulation results, where the degree distribution is proportional to l^{-1}. The reason for this difference seems to be that these simulations are based on different distributions of nodes.

Another earlier study by Manna and Kabakcioglu [8] notes that the link distance distribution has a stretched exponential tail for a scale-free network with the shortest total link length. This result is different from ours and from Yook's and Waxman's. However, this earlier study assumes that nodes are equally distributed within a square on a plane, and it seems that this assumption can generate differences in the results. Therefore, we cannot immediately say that a joint application network and the Internet have a tendency for redundancy in link length, and we need to investigate this carefully in the future.

7.4 Discussion

This chapter analysed the degree distribution, node density distribution, and link distance distribution of a cooperative R&D network and presented the capabilities of a model to reproduce a network that is similar to the original network with these distributions. However, there are other measures, e.g. clustering coefficients, degree correlations, and betweenness, for analysing networks. The model in this chapter may not reproduce a similar network in terms of these other measurements. Indeed, joint applications must be based on complex conditions; models that only use degrees and link distances do not necessarily reproduce precise network structures. Therefore, further improvement is desired.

There is another limitation to the model. Intuitively, it seems that organizations would want to increase their links to others. However, this model cannot indicate a strategy to increase the number of links, although it can show where new links could probably be created. This should be further developed in future studies.

Even with these limitations, the findings in this chapter can be interpreted as follows. The degree distribution is one of the most basic measures because it reveals the existence of hubs of various sizes. The link distance distribution is also important because policies such as supporting industrial clusters are based on the concept of geographical aggregation. Since the model discussed in this chapter can reproduce these two important structures of networks, it is useful for policy making.

As previously discussed, the requirements to balance degrees and link distances in probability reveal that neither factor has an extreme effect on the other. Because locations can be more easily controlled than the number of links, a firm that does not have R&D ability could compensate for its shortage of links by exploiting the distances between offices.

References

1. Barabási AL, Albert R. Emergence of scaling in random networks. Science. 1999;286:509–12.
2. Barabási AL, Oltvai ZN. Network biology: understanding the cell's functional organization. Nat Rev Genet. 2004;5:101–13.
3. Caldarelli G, et al. Scale-free networks from varying vertex intrinsic fitness. Phys Rev Lett. 2002;89(25):258702.
4. Clauset A, Shalizi CR, Newman MEJ. Power-law distributions in empirical data; 2007. arXiv:0706.1062.
5. Inoue H, Souma W, Tamada S. Spatial characteristics of joint application networks in Japanese patents. Phys A. 2007;383:152–7.
6. Inoue H, Souma W, Tamada S. Analysis of cooperative research and development networks on Japanese patents. J Info. 2010;4(1):89–96.
7. Krapivsky PL, Rendner S. Organization of growing random networks. Phys Rev E. 2001;63:06123.
8. Manna SS, Kabakcioglu A. Scale-free network on Euclidean space optimized by rewiring of links. J Phys A Math Gen. 2003;36(19):L279–85.
9. Manna SS, Sen P. Modulated scale-free network in the Euclidean space. Phys Rev E. 2002;66:066114.
10. Tamada S, et al. Significant difference of dependence upon scientific knowledge among different technologies. Scientometrics. 2006;68(2):289–302.
11. Waxman BM. Routing of multipoint connections. IEEE J Sel Areas Commun. 1988;6(9):1617–22.
12. Yook S, Jeong H, Barabási AL. Modeling the internet's large-scale topology. Proc Natl Acad Sci. 2002;99(21):13382–86.

Chapter 8
Generative Model: Intertexture of Firm and Inventor

8.1 Introduction

Chapter 7 described a model to replicate the joint application network that considers the degree and distance of establishments. However, collaborative activities are performed by inventors. Therefore, networks at the establishment or firm level are aggregations of inventors' collaborative activities. Since inventors are certainly affected by the organizations they belong to and the networks that these organizations form, considering either inventors' or organizations' networks in isolation may have the limitation of replicating the other networks. This chapter discusses overlapping networks and a model to replicate them, based on a study previously published by the author [11]. The figures and tables are replicated with proper permission from the publisher. The main text is modified to fit the context of this book.

As previously discussed, actors working collaboratively can create higher-quality works than can individual actors in isolation, [25] and inter-organizational work has a greater impact than intra-organizational work [13]. Therefore, it is important to know how such collaborative works are created. To this end, models to replicate these networks, i.e. generative models for collaboration networks, are discussed in the literature [1, 18, 19, 22] and in Chap. 7. However, all of these are models of one-layer networks.

Collaborations taking place through firms are conducted by individuals (i.e. developers or researchers) belonging to the firms. However, individuals seem to be affected by past collaborations between firms. There thus appears to be interdependency between individual and firm networks.

Here, we propose a model of two-layer networks, where the upper networks are expressed by aggregations of nodes and links belonging to lower networks. This model replicates networks from Japanese and the US patent data in terms of degree distributions.

H. Inoue, *Co-patenting: An Analytic Tool for Cooperative Research and Development*, Evolutionary Economics and Social Complexity Science 21,
https://doi.org/10.1007/978-4-431-54807-2_8

Although previous studies [4] have investigated two-layered networks, the model proposed here can better replicate the observed data with respect to degree distributions than previous models. Additionally, our model uses only local information, while other models have to use overall information, which is an unrealistic set-up in complex networks.

8.2 Data

This chapter uses patent data from Japan (JP) and the United States [10, 23]. We need the identifications (IDs) of rights holders and inventors to conduct this analysis. Assigning IDs to the rights holders is easy because their names and addresses provide sufficient information. Firms are extracted from the rights holders based on their names. The corporate statuses in the rights holders' names are used to extract this the information in the JP data set. The US data set already contains this information.

In contrast, inventors are identified by name, address, and firm. Assigning IDs to inventors requires an additional process when using patent data. The original patent data lack IDs. A comprehensive study has been conducted to develop such an identification process [24] that considers names, addresses, affiliations, co-inventors, technological classifications, citations, and different spellings of names. However, the primary aim of this detailed process is to net out the movements of inventors. Our analysis does not consider their movements. Thus, it is sufficient to identify inventors by their names, addresses, and affiliations.

Figure 8.1 plots the cumulative probabilities of the number of patents per inventor. The Japanese and US data have similar patterns. After identification,

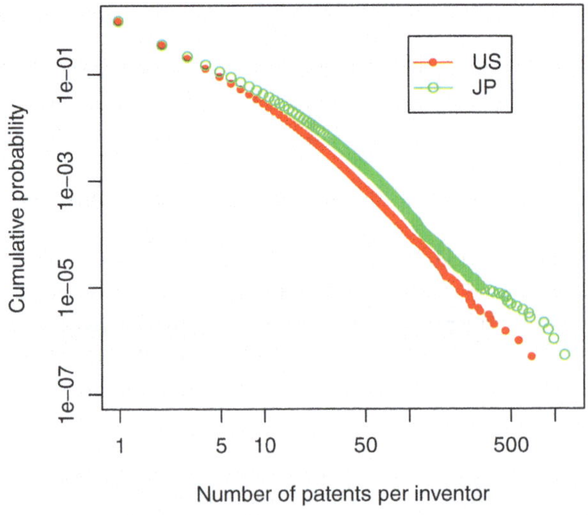

Fig. 8.1 Cumulative probability of the number of patents per inventor: the horizontal axis plots the number of patents per inventor, and the vertical axis plots the cumulative probability. Japan and the United States have similar patterns. (Source: [11])

4,649,617 names in patents are assigned to a total of 1,806,259 inventors in Japan, and 4,301,229 names are assigned to 1,923,241 inventors in the United States.

Another process is conducted to connect each inventor with a firm. An inventor is connected to a firm if (1) the inventor can be found on a patent applied for by a firm, or (2) the inventor can be found in patents jointly applied for by more than one firm, and there is only one common firm in the firms. Since most Japanese inventors' addresses contain firm names, we also use this information.

It is common for teams of inventors to apply for patents, and such patents have a considerably better impact (more citations) than those authored by solo inventors [25]. However, it is less common for more than one firm to jointly apply for patents. This is because no firm can sell or license a patent that is jointly applied for without the consent of the others. Additionally, joint applications are more costly than other solutions, such as solo applications with contracts for benefit sharing, and consequently, joint applications between firms are considered "second best" [9]. The number of patents jointly applied for by multiple firms account for 1.5% of all patents in the United States and 7.8% in Japan.

Table 8.1 summarizes the fundamental data from the two data sets with the number of patents, inventors, and firms. Figure 8.2 shows how two-layer networks are created from the data sets. The left of Fig. 8.2 shows an example for three patents, five inventors, and three firms. One or more inventors apply for a patent, and each inventor works for a firm. On the basis of the tripartite network on the left, we can create two different projected networks for the inventors and the firms. The inventor network is a network in which every combination of inventors has a link if they have at least one patent in common. The firm network is defined analogously. If inventors who apply for a patent belong to different firms, the firms have a link.

Figure 8.3 plots the cumulative probability degree distributions. "Original" consists of the plots for the observed data. The other plots are the results of models explained below. The figure plots the inventor and firm networks for JP and the United States. The figure indicates that the distributions of inventors decay faster than dictated by a power law. Previous studies have found that collaboration networks have the same distributions as those in this chapter [8, 18] or power laws [2]. The plots of the firm networks seem to be linear, i.e. power-law distributions.

Table 8.1 Overview of data sets: The range of years in which patents were applied for is labeled "Duration". The table lists the numbers of patents and firms that are included in the patents. Inventors working for firms are extracted. (Source: [11])

	US	JP
Duration (year)	1963–1999	1994–2008
Total number of patents	2,923,922	1,967,361
Number of firms	33,515	72,841
Number of inventors in firms	285,418	829,052
Number of patents by multiple inventors	347,450	1,043,639
Total number of patents by firms	722,350	1,696,635
Number of patents by multiple firms	28,345	132,704

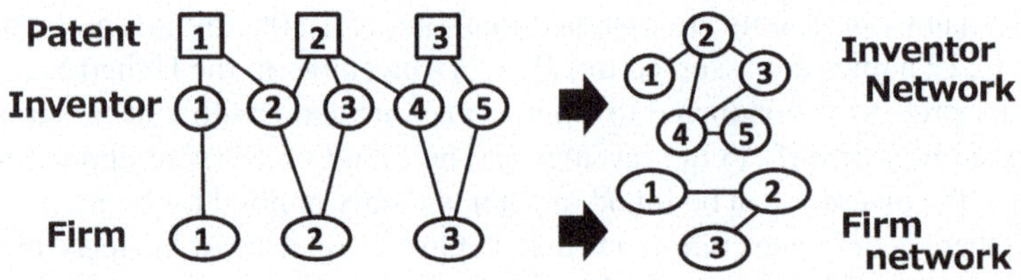

Fig. 8.2 Process to create two-layer networks from observed data: the figure shows how two different networks are created from patent data. A patent can be applied for by two or more inventors. Additionally, a patent can be applied for by two or more firms. For example, patent 1 has two inventors, 1 and 2. These inventors are connected in the inventor network. The inventors belong to firms 1 and 2, respectively. Therefore, firms 1 and 2 are connected. (Source: [11])

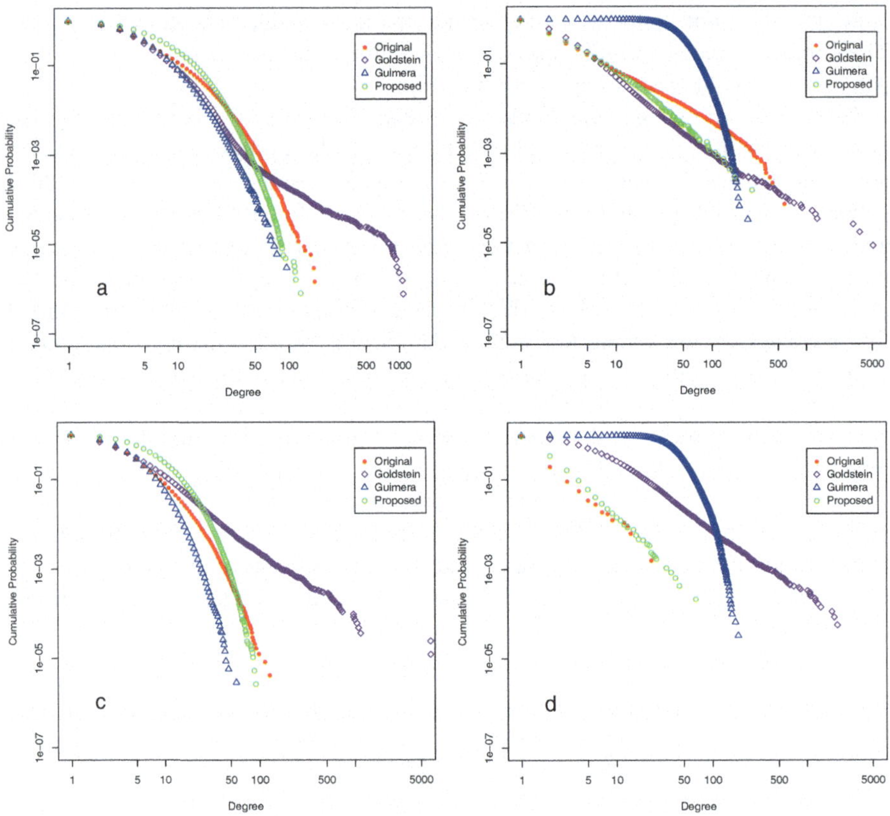

Fig. 8.3 Cumulative probability distributions for the degree of inventor and firm networks. "Original" is the observed data. "Goldstein", "Guimera", and "Proposed" are the data derived from each model with parameters obtained from the simulated annealing. (**a**) Japanese inventors (**b**) Japanese firms (**c**) US inventors (**d**) US firms. (Source: [11])

8.3 Model

On the basis of the observations thus far, we propose a model that replicates observed networks with respect to degree distributions.

This chapter focuses on two-layer networks that involve inventors and firms. To replicate the networks in this chapter, a generative model has to (1) explicitly assign a firm to each inventor in a replicated network and (2) replicate not only an inventor network but also a firm network.

Grönlund et al. proposed a modified seceder model to illustrate real social networks [7]. Jin et al.'s model is based on the dynamics whereby people actually meet [12]. Boguñá introduced the concept of social distance and identified models that could reproduce real social networks [3]. These models treat the formation of groups (firms in the present chapter) in observed networks and seem similar to the model that will be proposed here. However, they create networks of individuals and detect groups of individuals after creating individual networks [5, 20, 21]. This means that groups are not explicitly given. As previously mentioned, the model proposed here has to explicitly assign a group to each node (see item (1)). Therefore, these prior studies differ from the present work.

Some models assign groups to nodes beforehand when producing networks. Motter et al. considered the correlation of friendships, the positions in groups, and the correlation of positions in groups [17]. Kimura et al. demonstrated that their model improved the prediction of real networks by incorporating directional attachments and community structures [14]. These models seem similar to the model proposed below, but their organizational structures are given and do not grow (see item (2)).

Li and Chen also developed a theoretical model that satisfies both items (1) and (2). They showed that the degree distribution of the model exhibited a power law in both nodes and groups [16]. As explained in the previous section, the degree distributions of the inventors do not demonstrate a power law. Therefore, their model cannot be applied either.

This section reviewed relevant but inapplicable studies. Therefore, the following section presents two relevant models that have been proposed and serve as important comparisons for the model proposed in this chapter.

Goldstein et al.'s Model

Goldstein et al. proposed a model to replicate paper-author networks with groups of authors [6]. Their model satisfies both items (1) and (2) in the previous section. Note that they did not investigate structures of networks created between groups. Goldstein et al.'s model is comparable to the model proposed in this work.

Figure 8.4 is a diagram of their model. When a paper is written, there is a probability α that a new author group will be created with N_g new members,

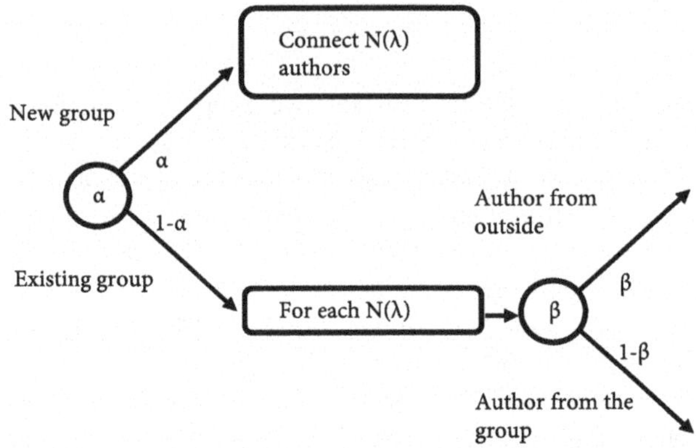

Fig. 8.4 Goldstein et al.'s model [6]: The process is repeated for every paper (or patents in this chapter). With probability α, a new group is created. The group has $N(\lambda)$ members. In other cases, an existing group is chosen. With probability β, an author is chosen from other groups. In other cases, an author is chosen from the group already chosen. When the choice is made, the author will be chosen in proportion to the number of times the author has been chosen in the past. (Source: [11])

where N_g is a constant. The number of authors of a paper, $N(\lambda)$, is the first author plus a Poisson-distributed number of additional authors. This one-shifted Poisson distribution has a parameter λ. The probability of the one-shifted Poisson distribution, $p_{\text{SP}}(k)$, is given by

$$p_{\text{SP}}(k) = \frac{\lambda^{(k-1)}e^{-\lambda}}{(k-1)!}, \quad k = \{1, 2, \ldots\}, \tag{8.1}$$

where k is the number of authors and $p_{\text{SP}}(k)$ is the probability of a paper having k authors.

If no new group is created, an existing author group is chosen using the following probability distribution:

$$p_g(q) = \frac{q}{N_p}, \tag{8.2}$$

where q is the number of papers that this group has published, N_p is the total number of papers in the network, and $p_g(q)$ is the probability of an existing group having authored a paper.

When adding each author, there is a probability β of choosing an author from another group. After choosing a group, the author is selected by using another preferential process. The probability of selecting author i for the group is

$$p_a(i) = \frac{k_i + 1}{\sum k_j + N_g}, \tag{8.3}$$

where k_i is the number of papers written by author i, $\sum k_j$ is the sum of the number of authorships of authors in the group, and N_g is the number of authors in the group.

Goldstein et al.'s model is simple and comparable to the model proposed here. However, note that Goldstein et al.'s model requires entire network information to calculate Eqs. (8.2) and (8.3). Obtaining entire network information is normally unrealistic because collaboration networks are vast and complex.

Guimera et al.'s Model

The model proposed in this chapter is based on Guimera et al.'s model [8], which is designed to replicate the self-assembly of creative teams and has two parameters: the fraction of newcomers in new projects (p) and the tendency of incumbents to repeat previous collaborations (q).

Figure 8.5 outlines the process of the model. The model has an endless pool of newcomers. Newcomers become incumbents after being selected. The model adds members to a team according to m. There are various ways of creating the sequence for m, e.g. hold m constant, or draw m from the observed distribution. The latter is used in this chapter. Probability p is that of a member being drawn from the pool of incumbents. If a member has already been chosen from the pool of incumbents and there is already another incumbent that is already connected but has not been chosen, a new member is chosen from the incumbents with probability q. Otherwise, a member is chosen from all the incumbents, regardless of team. The process is repeated m times for each team.

The Proposed Model

This chapter proposes a new model based on Guimera et al.'s model that can better replicate the two-layered networks obtained from the empirical data than the models

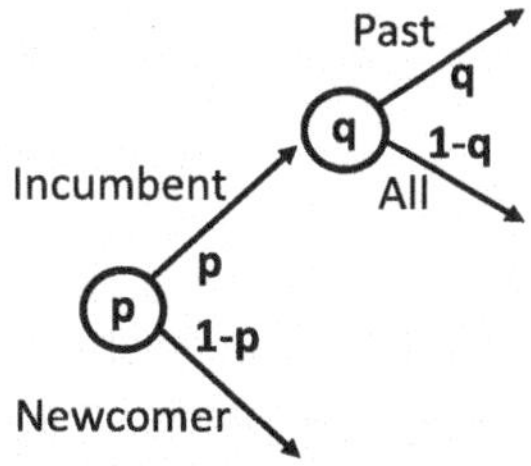

Fig. 8.5 Process in Guimera et al.'s model: the process is repeated for each member of a team. An incumbent is randomly chosen with probability p. If p is not true, a newcomer is created. After p is true, q is tested. With probability q, an incumbent is a past collaborator of the team's members. However, if q is not true, an incumbent is randomly chosen from all incumbents [8]. (Source: [11])

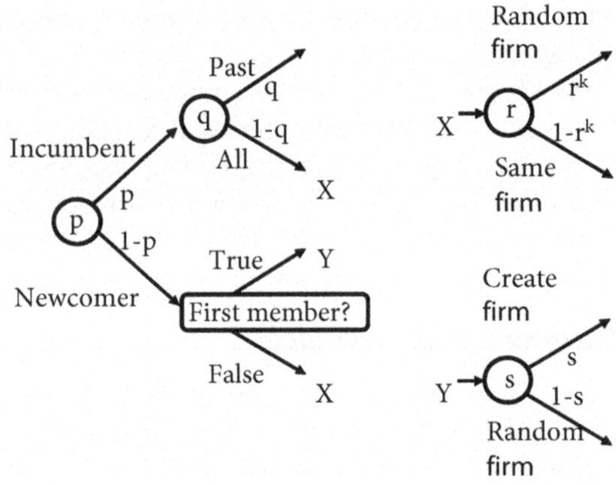

Fig. 8.6 Process of the proposed model: Guimera et al.'s model is presented at the top left. X and Y on the left indicate jumps to X and Y on the right. (Source: [11])

studied previously. Figure 8.6 outlines the proposed model. Guimera et al.'s model remains at the top left. The new model contains a new process for choosing firms (X) and creating firms (Y). There is a branch when an inventor is a newcomer. If the inventor is the first member of a team, Y is executed. If he or she is not, X is executed. X has a parameter, r. Here, r^k, where k is the number of firms already included in the patent, which is the probability of choosing a firm from the pool of all existing firms. Then, the newcomer or the incumbent is assigned to the chosen firm. If r^k is not true, a firm that one of the members already belongs to is chosen as the newcomer or the incumbent. Y has a parameter, s, which is the probability of creating a new firm. Then, the newcomer is assigned to the chosen firm. If s is not true, a firm is randomly chosen from the pool of all existing firms, and then the newcomer is assigned to it.

Simulation Results

Here, we consider Goldstein et al.'s, Guimera et al.'s, and our proposed model to replicate the two-layer networks observed in the empirical data to see how the proposed model improves replication compared to previous models. We perform the comparison after tuning the parameters of each model. The tuned parameters for Goldstein et al.'s model are α, β, λ, and N_g; those for Guimera et al.'s model are p and q; and those for the proposed model are p, q, r, and s.

The tuning is performed through *simulated annealings* [15]. The parameters are initially set to best match the values that can be obtained from the observed data.

The initial values of the parameters in Goldstein et al.'s model are $\alpha = 0.02$, $\beta = 0.17$, $\gamma = 1.53$, and $N_g = 26$ for Japanese data and $\alpha = 0.05$, $\beta = 0.28$, $\gamma = 0.6$, and $N_g = 9$ for the US data. The sizes of steps to search neighbourhoods in the simulated annealings are 0.01 for α and β, 0.1 for γ, and 1 for N_g. The following observed values are used as initial values. The probability with which new firms are found in patents is used as α. The average fraction of a firm's patents with inventors from an another firm is used as β. Since γ is a parameter of the one-shifted Poisson distribution, Eq. (8.1), γ can be obtained through least squares to fit the one-shifted Poisson distribution to the distribution of the number of authors. The average of the number of authors in patents is used as N_g.

Two parameters, p and q, which are necessary to run Guimera et al.'s model, are initially set at $p = 0.73$ and $q = 0.69$ for the Japanese data and $p = 0.78$ and $q = 0.66$ for the US data. The sizes of steps are 0.01 for p and q. We calculate the share of newcomers to members for every patent and the average share is used as p. We also calculate the share of repeated collaborations to all collaborations in every patent, and the average of these shares is used as q. In the simulation, each inventor is randomly assigned to a firm from a pool. The pool has the same number of firms as the observed data.

The new parameters in the proposed model, namely, r and s, are initially set at $r = 0.06$ and $s = 0.09$ for the Japanese data and as $r = 0.05$ and $s = 0.07$ for the US data. The size of steps is 0.01 for both r and s. We derive the probability distribution for a newcomer belonging to a firm other than the k firms already included in the patent. Then, we use least squares to set r for the distribution. s is set to the probability that a new inventor belongs to a new firm. The other initial settings are the same as those in the simulations of Guimera et al.'s model.

The simulated annealing creates and evaluates the networks 1,000 times. The probability of adopting worse parameters than the current parameters decays exponentially in the number of repetitions. Each repetition of the simulated annealing creates 1,696,635 patents to replicate the Japanese networks and 722,350 patents to replicate the US networks.

To evaluate the replicated networks, we use the Kolmogrov-Smirnov (KS) statistic, which indicates distances between two cumulative probability distributions. Here, two cumulative probability distributions are drawn from the obtained and replicated networks. Since there are two different networks to evaluate, i.e. inventor and firm networks, the sum of the KS statistics of the two networks is the value used for evaluation.

Table 8.2 lists the results of the parameter fitting. The "Total" column indicates the sums of the KS statistics of the inventor and firm networks, which are the values used to evaluate the simulated annealings. The table reports KS statistics for the inventor and firm's cumulative degree distributions for Goldstein et al.'s model, Guimera et al.'s model, and the proposed model. The smaller the KS statistic is, the closer two distributions drawn from a replicated and the observed networks are.

The total values for Guimera et al.'s model in Table 8.2 show that it is not comparable to the other models. The fitted parameters are $p = 0.92$ and $q = 0.93$ for the Japanese data and $p = 0.77$ and $q = 0.68$ for the US data. Although Guimera et al.'s model is able to replicate the inventor network well, it has large KS statistics for the firm network. Figure 8.3 also shows large deviations from the original firm network data. Since all inventors are randomly assigned to firms in the simulations, similar numbers of inventors are assigned to all firms. Therefore, the firm distribution does not match the observed distribution.

Table 8.2 Kolmogorov-Smirnov (KS) statistics after parameter fitting given by simulated annealings: Each number is a KS statistic between the distributions of a model and the observed distribution. A small KS statistic means that a distribution is close to the observed distribution. (Source: [11])

JP	Inventor	Firm	Total
Goldstein et al.'s model	0.05	0.12	0.17
Guimera et al.'s model	0.04	0.93	0.97
Proposed model	0.18	0.03	0.21
US	Inventor	Firm	Total
Goldstein et al.'s model	0.05	0.65	0.70
Guimera et al.'s model	0.03	0.98	1.01
Proposed model	0.23	0.13	0.46

On the other hand, Goldstein et al.'s model appears comparable to the proposed model. The fitted parameters are $\alpha = 0.18$, $\beta = 0.07$, $\lambda = 1.8$, and $N_g = 20$ for the Japanese data and $\alpha = 0, 06$, $\beta = 0.18$, $\lambda = 2.0$, and $N_g = 2$ for the US data. Its evaluation value for the Japanese data is superior to that of the proposed model (Table 8.2). However, we observe substantial deviations from the observed data on the inventor network in Fig. 8.3. This is because KS statistics are absolute values, and they place less weight on the evaluation of the tails of distributions. This substantial deviation in the tails shows that Goldstein et al.'s model does not seem to outperform the proposed model.

The proposed model appears to be better able to replicate the observed networks, although it does not always exhibit better performance than Goldstein et al.'s model with respect to the KS statistics. Figure 8.3 demonstrates that the proposed model does not have as substantial of a deviation as the other models. The fitted parameters are $p = 0.64$, $q = 0.65$, $r = 0.10$, and $s = 0.25$ for the Japanese data and $p = 0.43$, $q = 0.60$, $r = 0.03$, and $s = 0.28$ for the US data. Note that the proposed model does not require all of the network information but that Goldstein et al.'s model does. Since obtaining entire information about a network is unrealistic, this is advantage of the proposed model.

8.4 Discussion

This chapter attempted to clarify the interdependency between inventor and firm networks using patent data from Japan and the United States. Additionally, two different networks were created from tripartite graphs of patents, firms, and inventors. We proposed a model to replicate two-layer networks to understand the interdependent evolution of these networks. The model is based on Guimera et al.'s model and is better able to replicate the observed networks in terms of cumulative degree distributions. A key characteristic of the proposed model is that all processes only use local information, which is not the case for the other models.

Since the model better replicates the degree distributions of inventors and firms than the other models, the characteristics of the proposed model may help to understand the mechanism by which inventors and firms select partners. The following three characteristics can be deduced from the proposed model. (1) Inventors with many connections to other inventors are more likely to obtain additional connections in the future; since the fit results showed that p and q have large values, the path consisting of p and q (Fig. 8.6) often happens. Therefore, an inventor with many links is likely to be involved in a team. (2) Firms with many inventors can acquire inter-firm connections; a new connection between firms can mainly be obtained from the path where p is true, q is false, and r^k is true. Since an incumbent is randomly chosen in the process, a firm with many incumbents is likely to be chosen. (3) Groups of inter-firm connections grow by attracting new connections to the existing inter-firm connections; as mentioned in (1), the path consisting of p and q often happens. If there is an inter-firm team, other inventors tend to be involved in the team. Therefore, inter-firm links are likely to increase.

However, the proposed model does not truly replicate the observed data because it cannot pass statistically strict tests, such as a KS test. However, no other models, even for one-layer networks, seem to be able to replicate true distributions. Therefore, the proposed model can be considered a basis for creating a better model in the future.

References

1. Barabási AL, Albert R. Statistical mechanics of complex networks. Rev Mod Phys. 2002;74:47–97.
2. Barabási AL, et al. Evolution of the social network of scientific collaborations. Phys A. 2002;311:590–614.
3. Boguñá M, et al. Models of social networks based on social distance attachment. Phys Rev E. 2004;70(5):1–8. 1
4. Chessa A, et al. Is Europle evolving toward an integrated research area? Science. 2013;339(6120):650–1.
5. Girvan M, Newman MEJ. Community structure in social and biological networks. Proc Natl Acad Sci USA. 2002;99(12):7821–26.
6. Goldstein M, Morris S, Yen G. Group-based Yule model for bipartite author-paper networks. Phys Rev E. 2005;71(2):1–6.
7. Grönlund A, Holme P. Networking the seceder model: group formation in social and economic systems. Phys Rev E. 2004;70(3):1–9.
8. Guimera R, et al. Team assembly mechanisms determine collaboration network structure and team performance. Science. 2005;308(5722):697–702.
9. Hagedoorn J, Kranenburg HV, Osborn RN. Joint patenting amongst companies – exploring the effects of inter-firm R&D partnering and experience. Manag Decis Econ. 2003;24:71–84.
10. Hall BH, Jaffe AB, Trajtenberg M. The NBER patent citations data file: lessons, insights and methodological tools. National Bureau of Economic Research Working Paper 8498; 2001.
11. Inoue H. A two-layer team-assembly model for invention networks. Phys A Stat Mech Appl. 2014;415:181–8.
12. Jin EM, Girvan M, Newman ME. Structure of growing social networks. Phys Rev E. 2001;64(4):046132.

13. Jones BJ, Wuchty S, Uzzi B. Multi-university research teams: shifting impact, geography, and stratification in science. Science. 2008;322(5905):1259–62.
14. Kimura M, Saito K, Ueda N. Modeling of growing networks with directional attachment and communities. Neural Netw. 2004;17(7):975–88.
15. Kirkpatrick S, Gelatt Jr CC, Vecchi MP. Optimization by simulated annealing. Science. 1983;220(4598):671–80.
16. Li C, Maini PK. An evolving network model with community structure. J Phys A Math Gen. 2005;38(45):9741–9.
17. Motter A, Nishikawa T, Lai Y-C. Large-scale structural organization of social networks. Phys Rev E. 2003;68(3):1–5.
18. Newman MEJ. The structure of scientific collaboration networks. Proc Natl Acad Sci USA. 2001;98:404–9.
19. Newman MEJ. Coauthorship networks and patterns of scientific collaboration. Proc Natl Acad Sci USA. 2004;101:5200–5.
20. Newman MEJ, Girvan M. Finding and evaluating community structure in networks. Phys Rev E. 2004;69(2):1–5.
21. Radicchi F, et al. Defining and identifying communities in networks. Proc Natl Acad Sci USA. 2004;101(9):2658–63.
22. Ramasco J, Dorogovtsev S, Pastor-Satorras R. Self-organization of collaboration networks. Phys Rev E. 2004;70(30):1–10.
23. Tamada S, Kodama F, Gemba K. A study on science linkage of Japanese patents; an analysis on patents in the field of genetic technology by constructing a citation database. J Sci Policy Res Manag. 2002;17(3/4):222–30.
24. Trajtenberg M, Shiff G, Melamed R. The "NAMES GAME": harnessing inventors' patent data for economic research. National Bureau of Economic Research Working Paper 12479; 2006.
25. Wuchty S, Jones BF, Uzzi B. The increasing dominance of teams in production of knowledge. Science. 2007;316(5827):1036–9.

The manufacturer's authorised representative in the EU is Springer Nature Customer Service Centre GmbH, Europaplatz 3, 69115 Heidelberg, Germany. If you have any concerns regarding our products, please contact ProductSafety@springernature.com

Printed and bound by CPI Group (UK) Ltd, Croydon, CR0 4YY
25/09/2026
02222892-0015